Contents

PIANO CLASSICS

68 MASTERWORKS FOR THE KEYBOARD

Amsco Publications
A Part of **The Music Sales Group**
New York/London/Paris/Sydney/Copenhagen/Berlin/Tokyo/Madrid

Poem

Zdeněk Fibich
(1850–1900)

Slowly, with expression

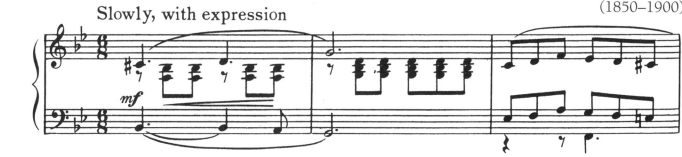

Malagueña

Isaac Albéniz
(1860–1909)

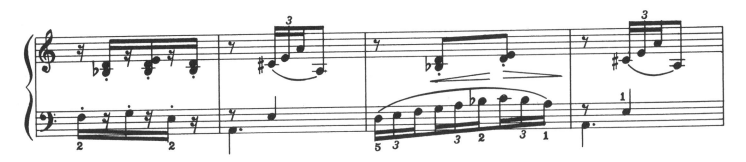

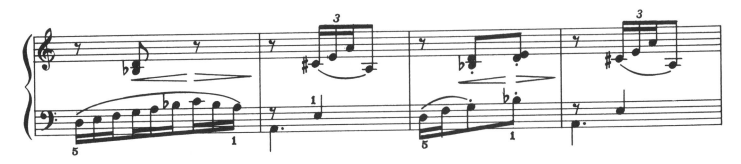

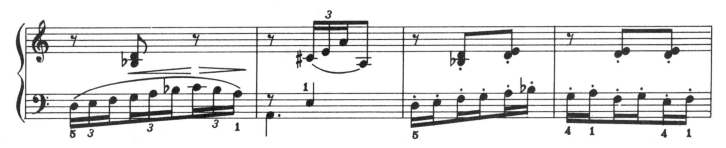

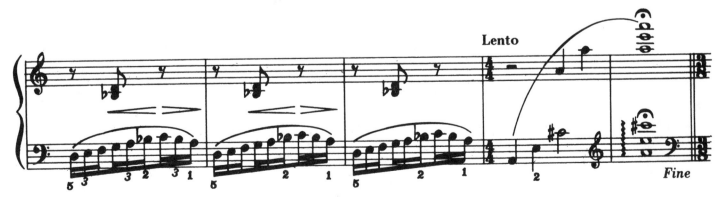

Dal 𝄋 al Fine

9

Four Pieces From Little Notebook
Minuet

Johann Sebastian Bach
(1685–1750)

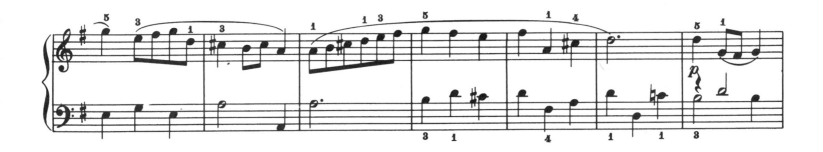

Minuet

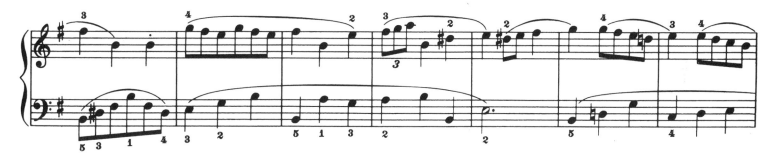

Musette

March

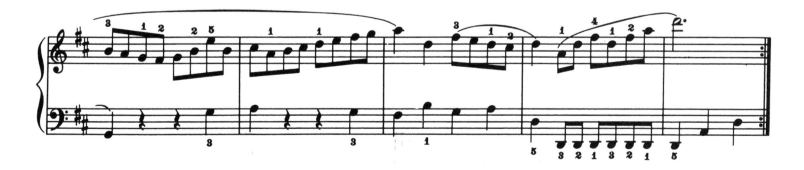

Prelude No. 1

from The Well-Tempered Clavier Book 1

Johann Sebastian Bach
(1685–1750)

Prelude and Fugue No. 12

from The Well-Tempered Clavier Book 2

Prelude

Johann Sebastian Bach
(1685–1750)

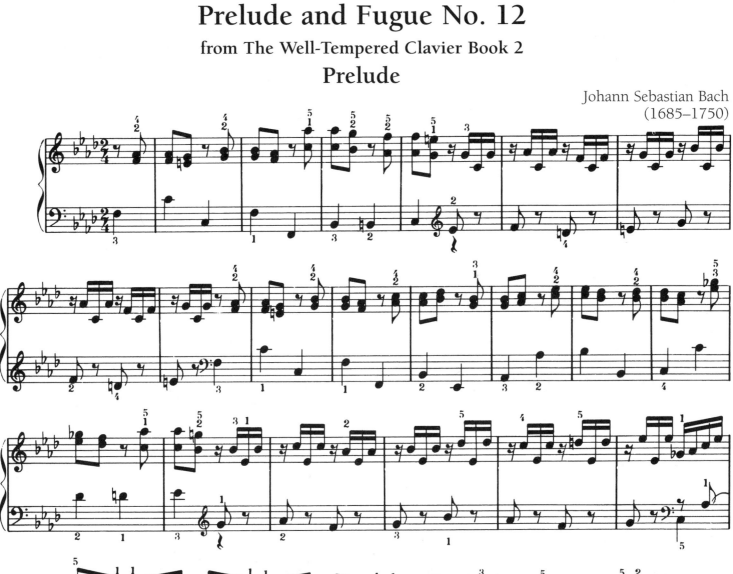

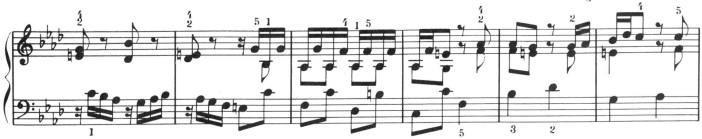

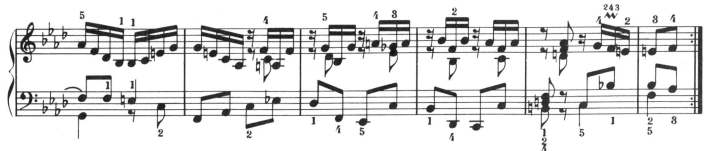

Fugue

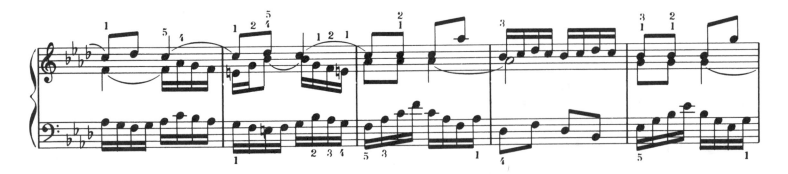

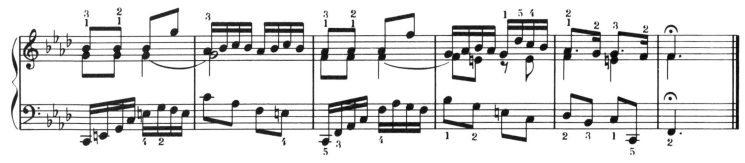

Prelude and Fugue No. 2

from The Well-Tempered Clavier Book 1

Prelude

Johann Sebastian Bach
(1685–1750)

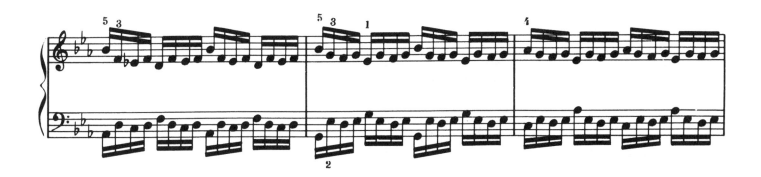

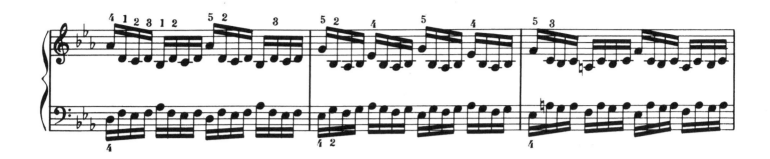

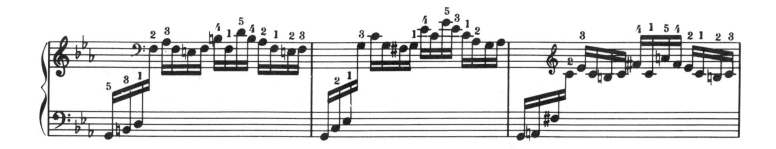

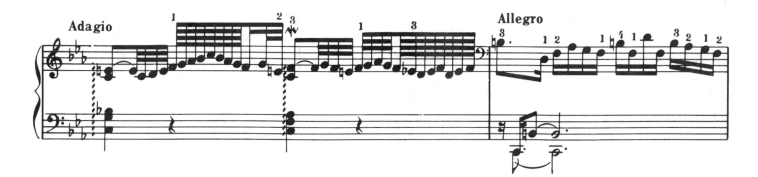

Fugue

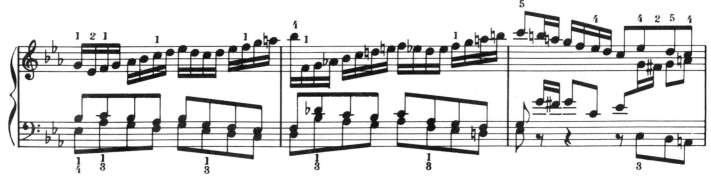

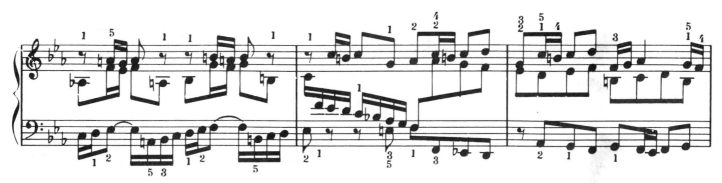

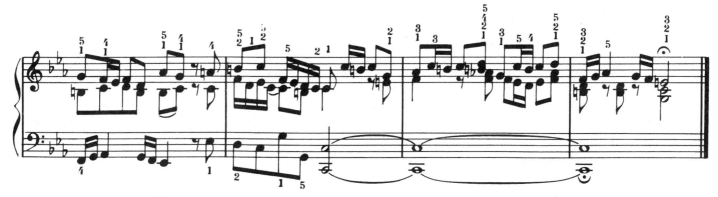

Air

from Suite in D Major

Johann Sebastian Bach
(1685–1750)

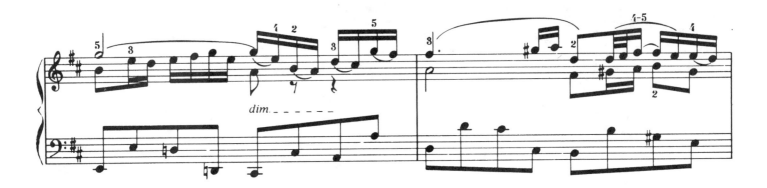

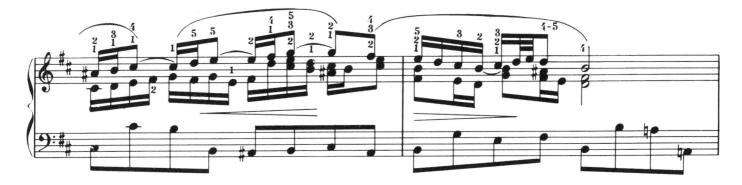

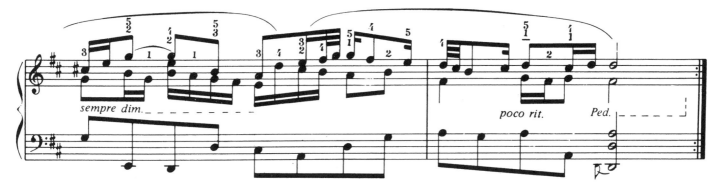

Bagatelle

Ludwig van Beethoven
(1770–1827)

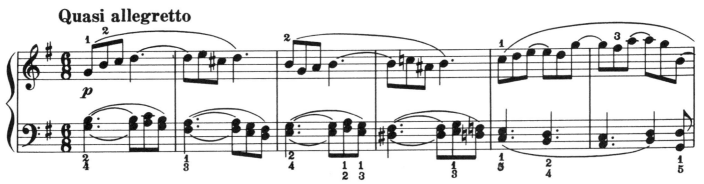

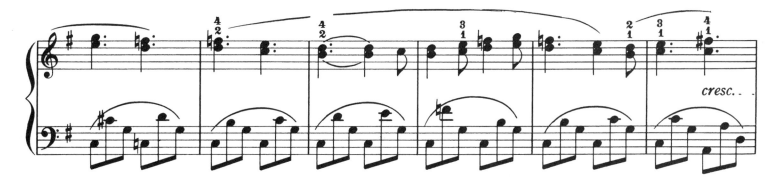

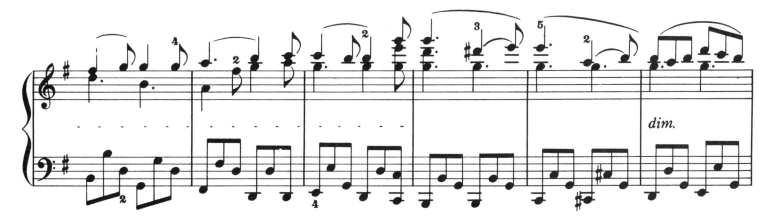

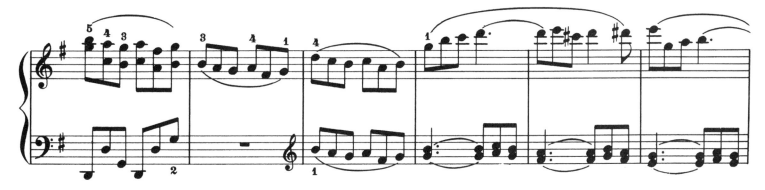

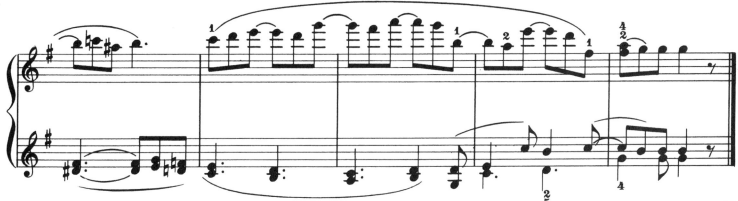

Ecossaises

Ludwig van Beethoven
(1770–1827)

NOTE: *Arranged for Concert Performance by Ferruccio Busoni*

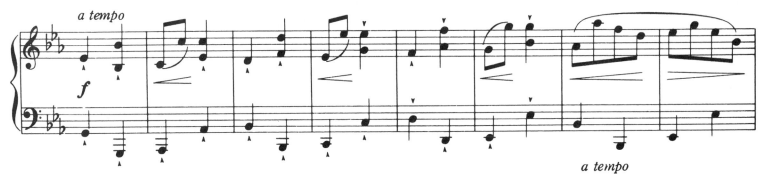

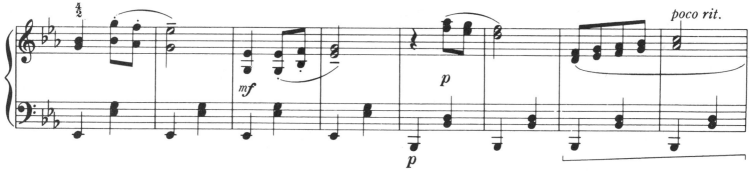

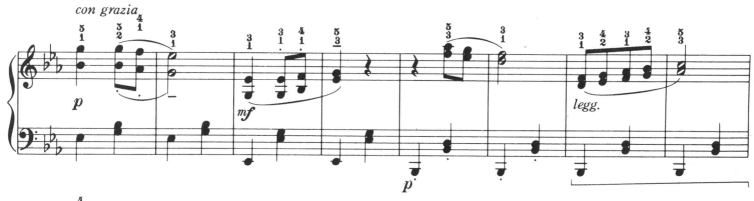

senza ped.

Tempo I

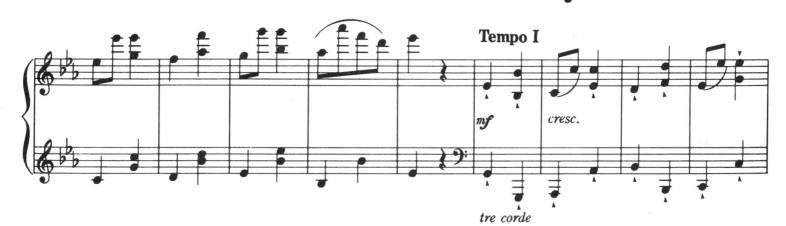

tre corde

Für Elise

Ludwig van Beethoven
(1770–1827)

Poco moto

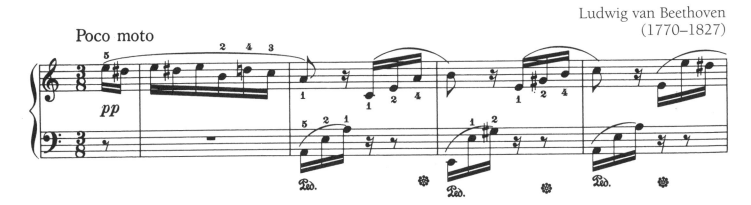

p cantando

legato

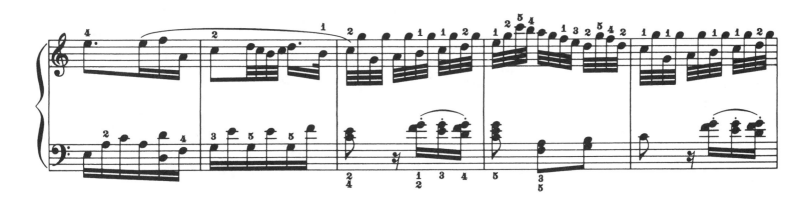

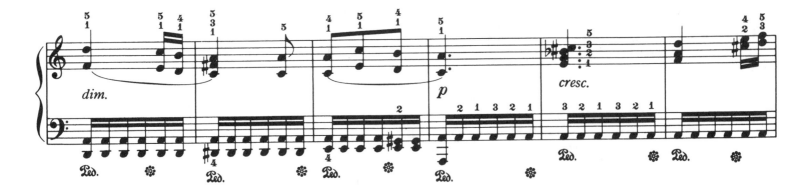

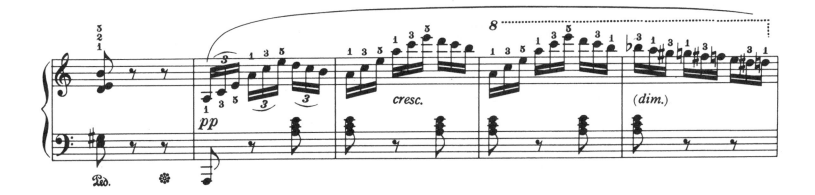

Minuet in G

Ludwig van Beethoven
(1770–1827)

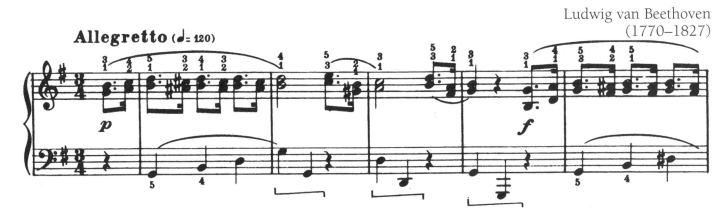

(p subito 2da volta)

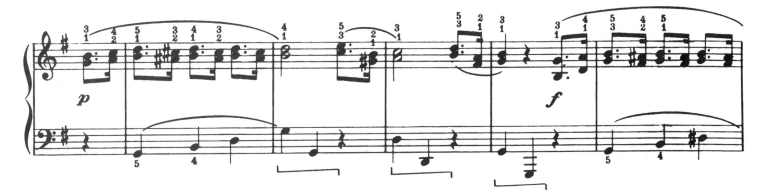

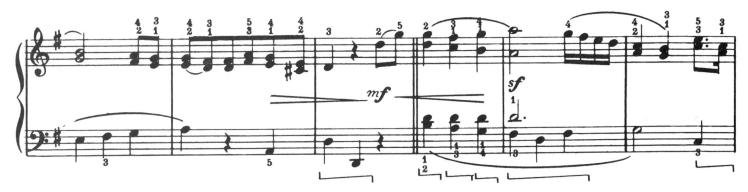

Moonlight Sonata

First Movement, Op. 27, No. 2

Ludwig van Beethoven
(1770–1827)

Six Variations

from the opera La Molinara

Ludwig van Beethoven
(1770–1827)

Andantino

Theme

Original title: *L'Amor contrastato*

Var. 1

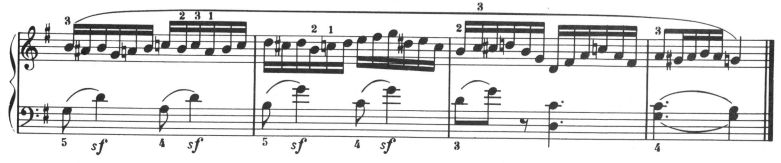

Var. 2

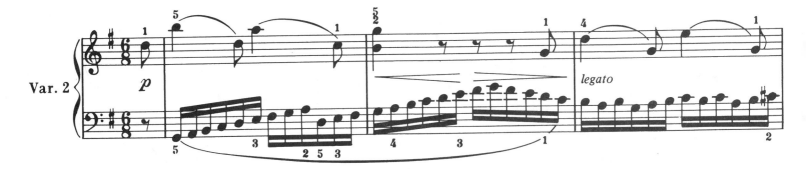

Var. 3

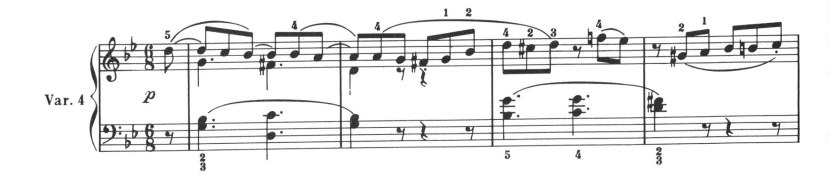

Var. 4

Var. 5

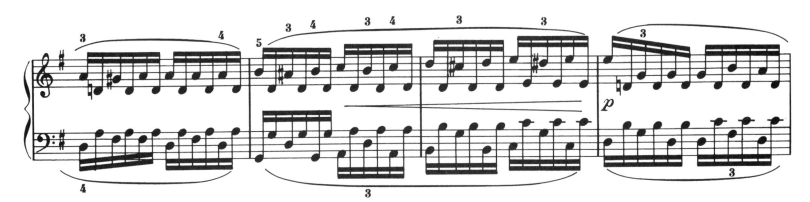

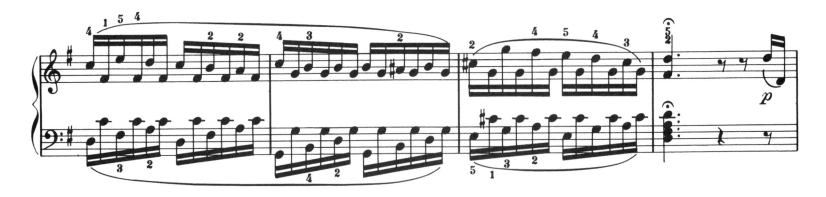

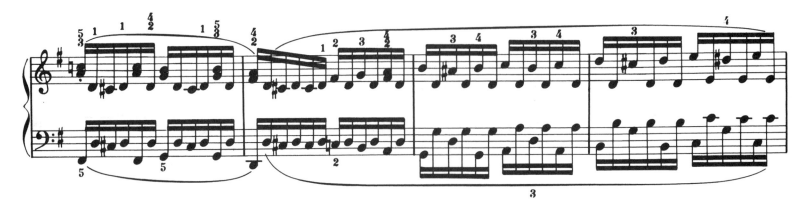

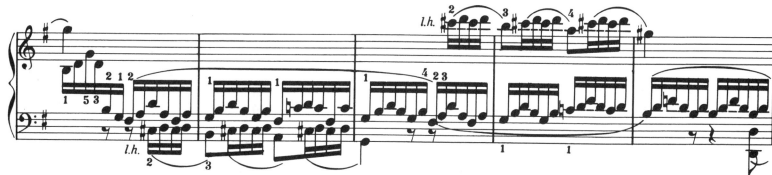

Waltz in A Flat

Op. 39, No. 15

Johannes Brahms
(1833–1897)

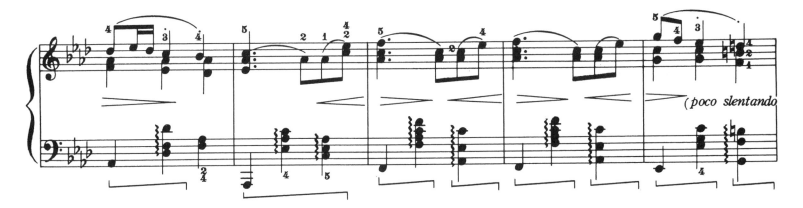

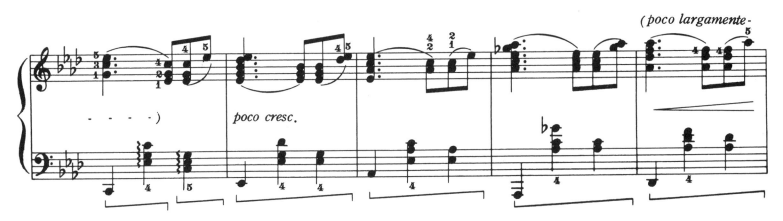

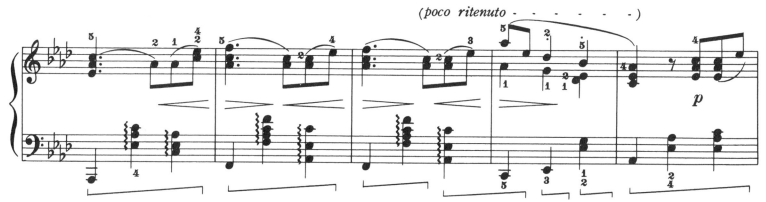

Hungarian Dance

No. 5

Johannes Brahms
(1833–1897)

Allegretto moderato

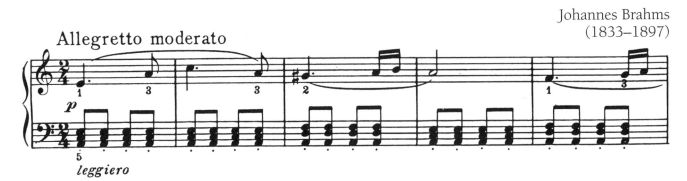

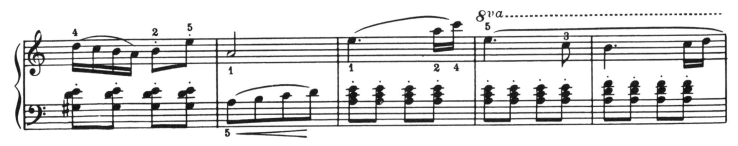

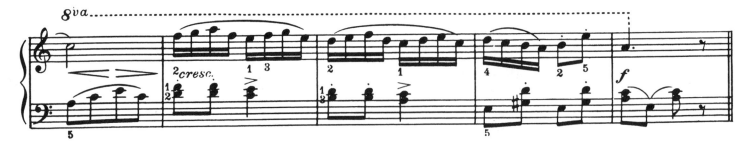

Meno mosso

2nd time to Coda

D.C. al %
poi CODA.

Coda

Fantasie-Impromptu

Frédéric Chopin
(1810–1849)

Largo

Moderato cantabile

a tempo

Valse

Op. 64, No. 2

Frédéric Chopin
(1810–1849)

Tempo guisto

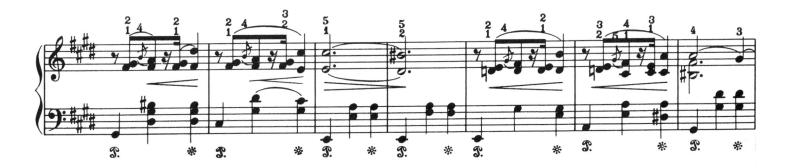

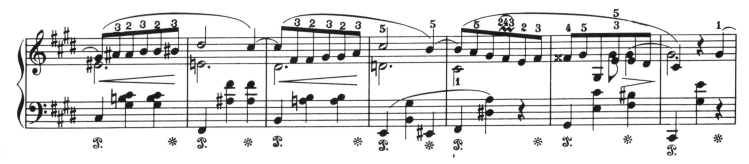

Più mosso

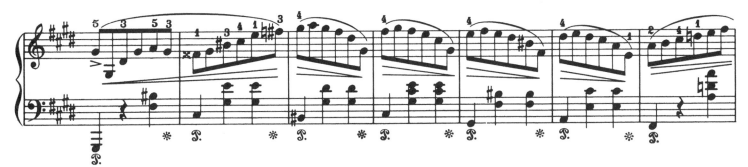

Più lento

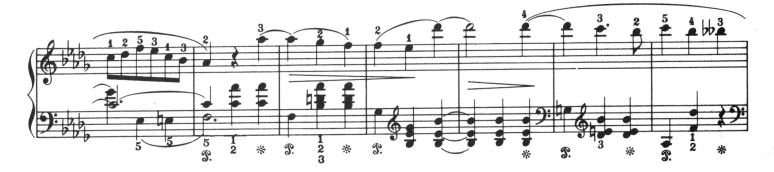

Più mosso

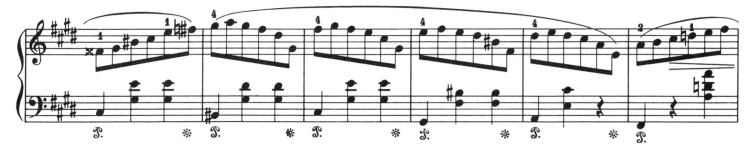

Tempo I

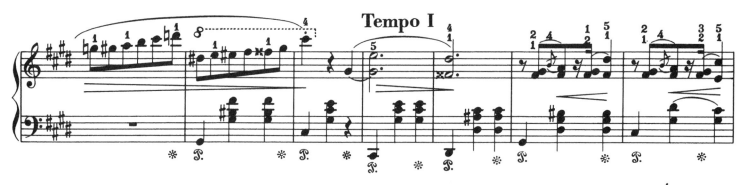

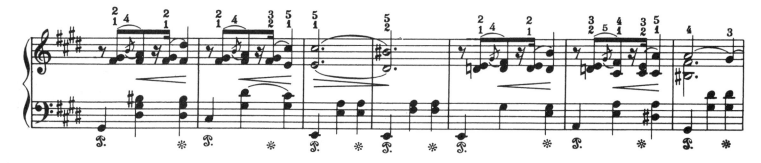

Più mosso

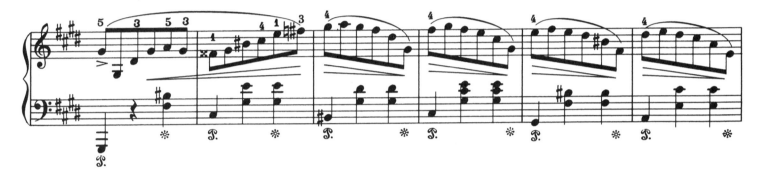

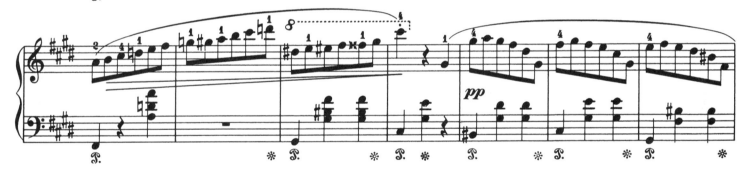

Nocturne
Op. 72, No. 1

Frédéric Chopin
(1810–1849)

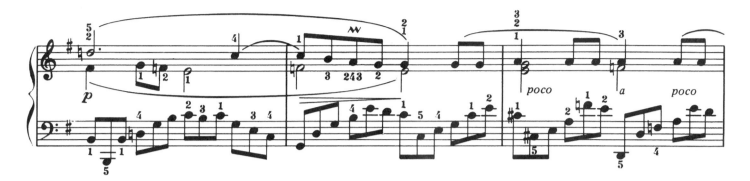

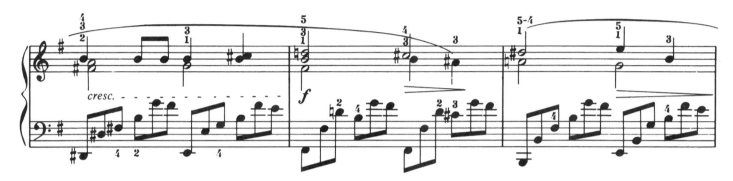

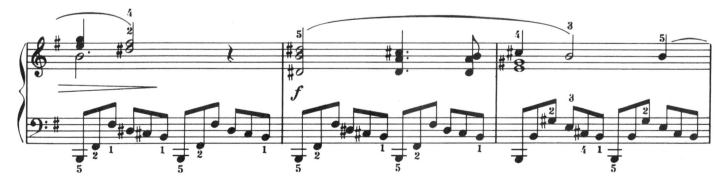

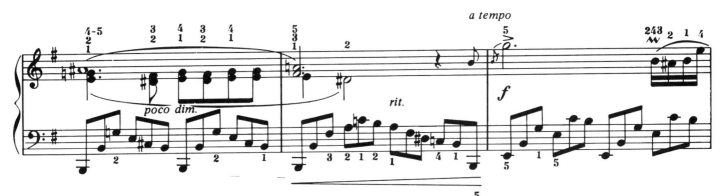

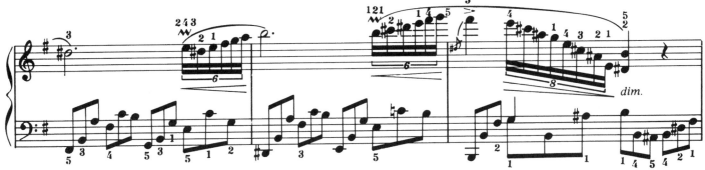

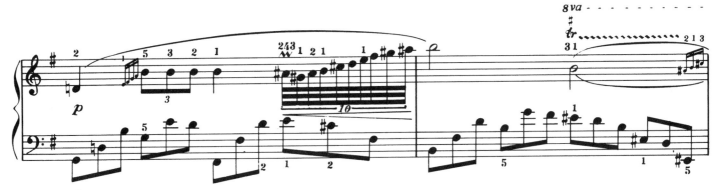

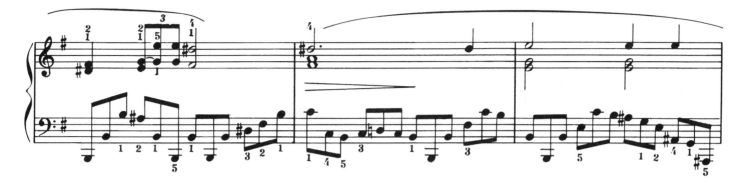

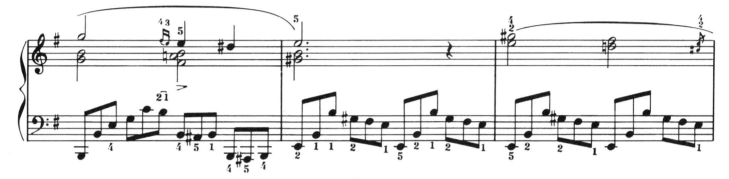

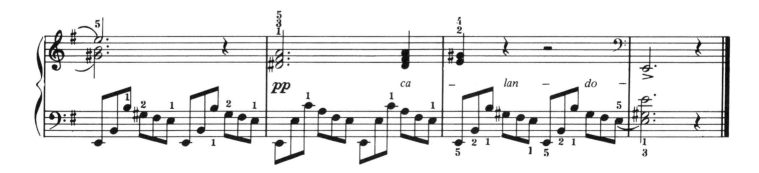

Prelude

Op. 28, No. 6

Frédéric Chopin
(1810–1849)

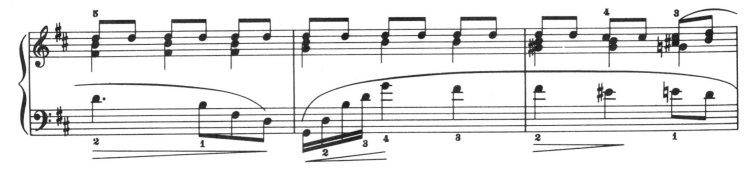

Prelude

Op. 28, No. 7

Frédéric Chopin
(1810–1849)

Andantino

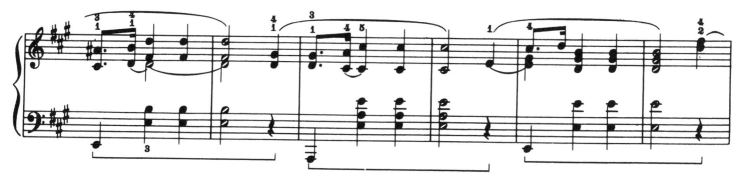

Mazurka in A minor

Op. 68, No. 2

Frédéric Chopin
(1810–1849)

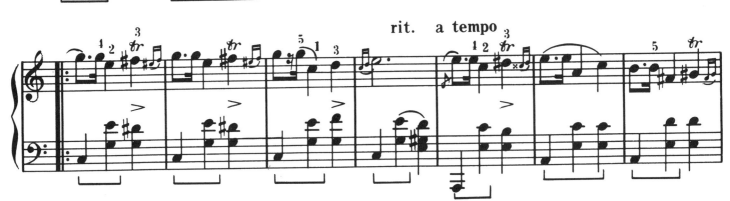

Mazurka in B Flat

Op. 7, No. 1

Frédéric Chopin
(1810–1849)

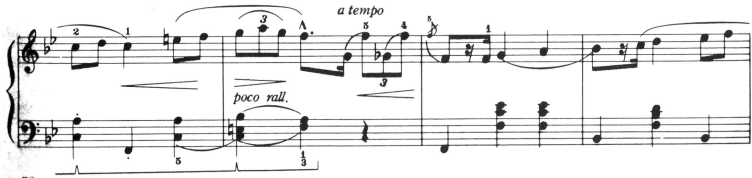

Nocturne

Posthumous

Frédéric Chopin
(1810–1849)

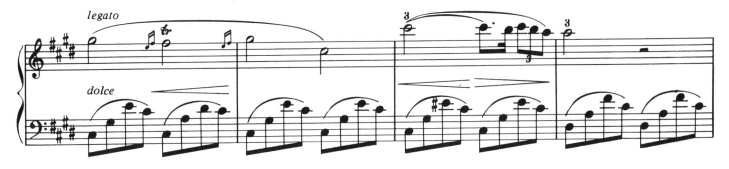

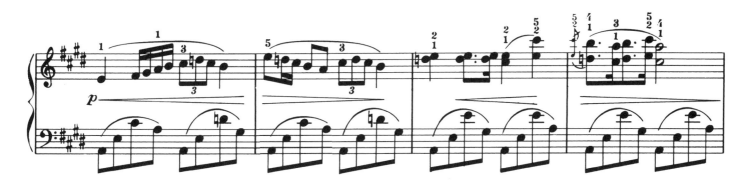

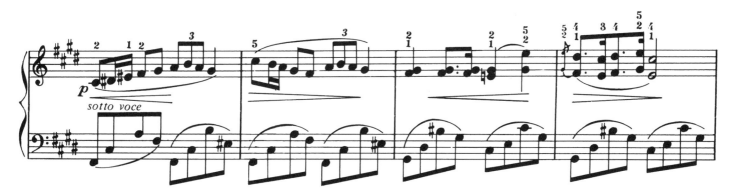

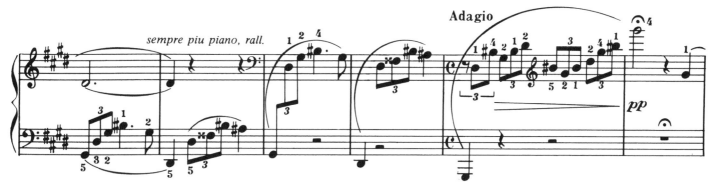

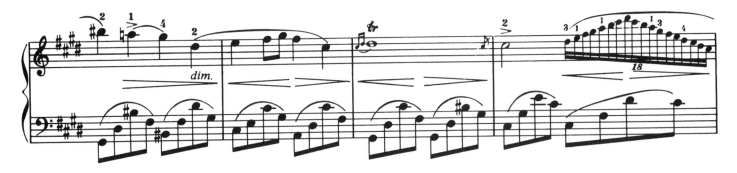

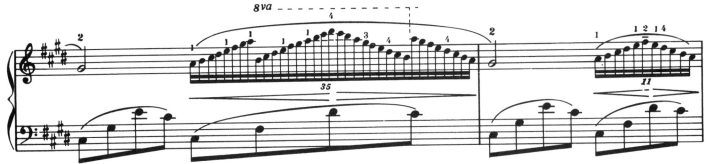

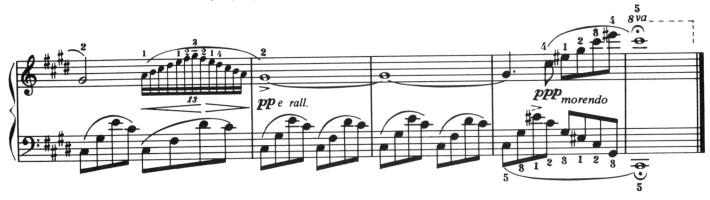

Valse

Op. 64, No. 1

Frédéric Chopin
(1810–1849)

Molto vivace

Le Coucou

Louis-Claude Daquin
(1694-1772)

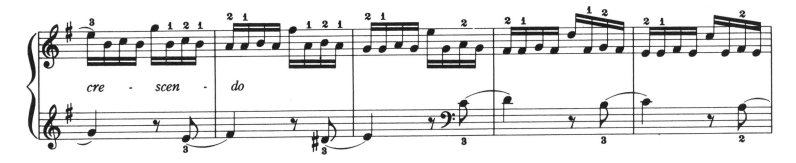

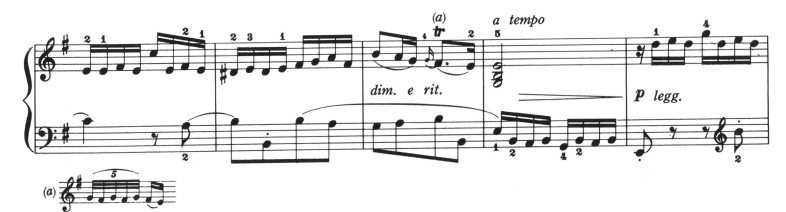

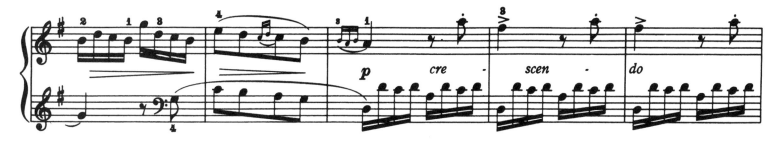

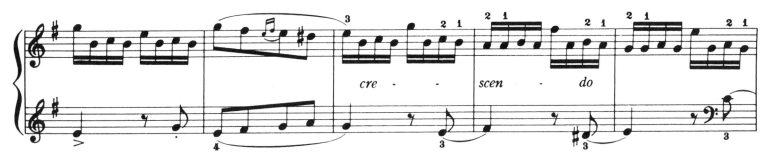

The Little Negro

Le Petit Negre

Claude Debussy
(1862–1918)

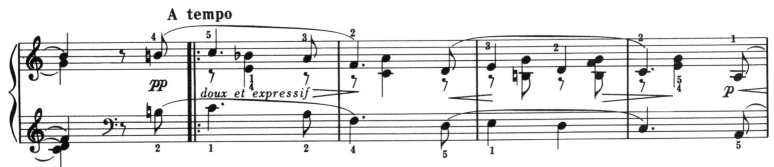

Clair de Lune

Claude Debussy
(1862–1918)

Andante très expressif

pp   con sordina

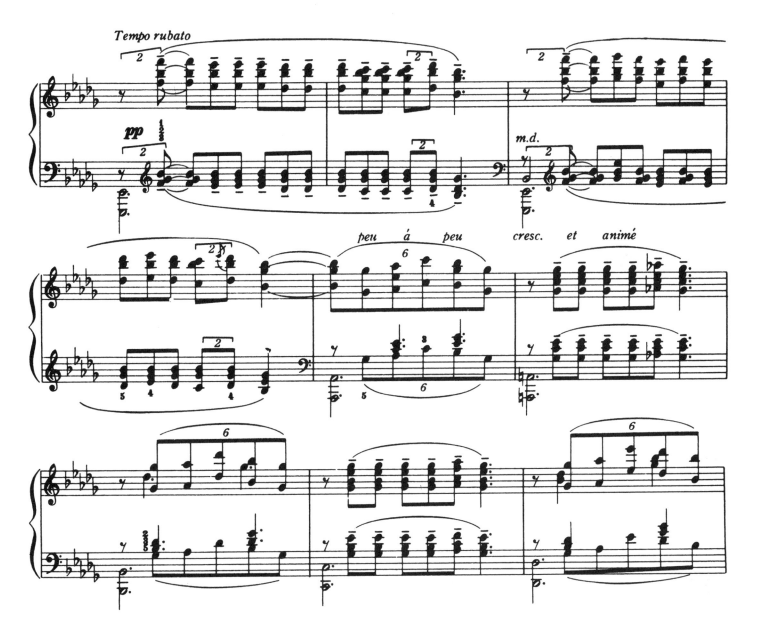

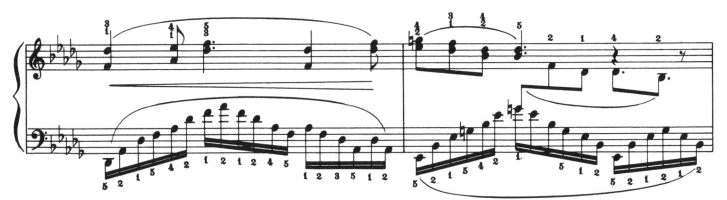

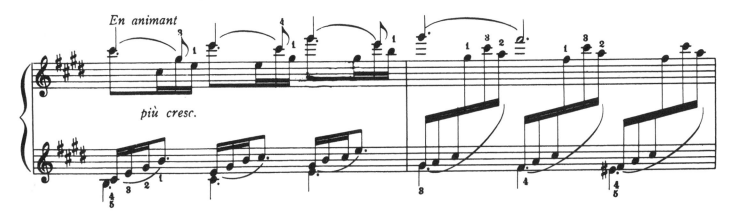

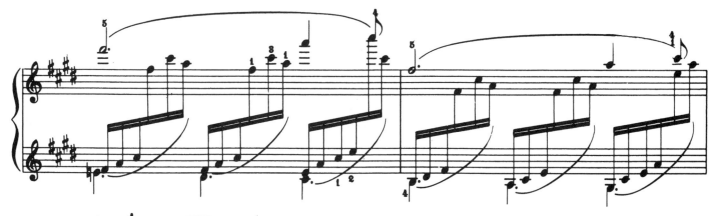

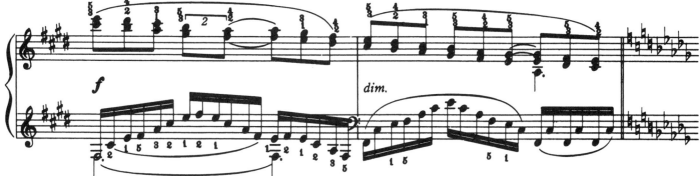

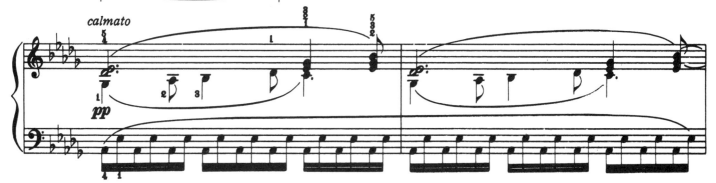

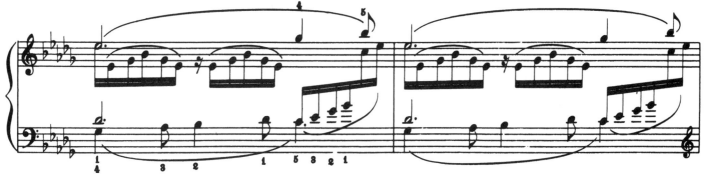

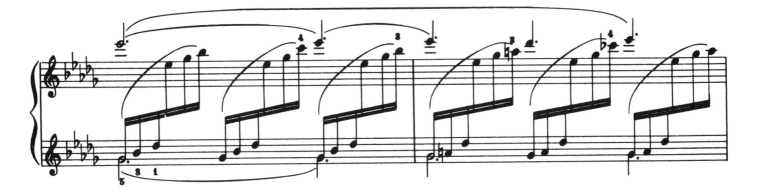

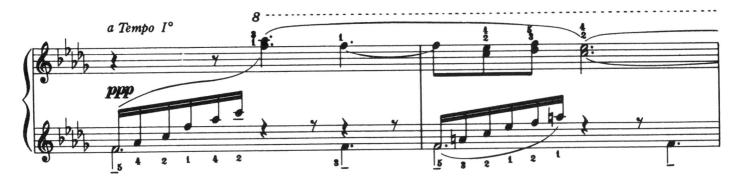

a Tempo I°

ppp

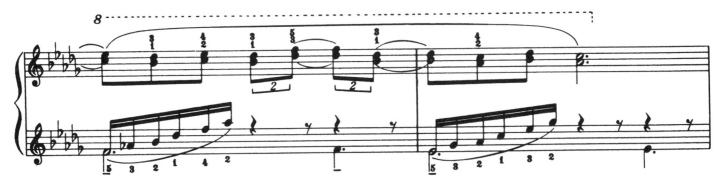

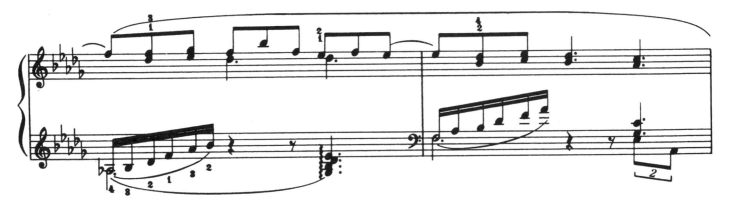

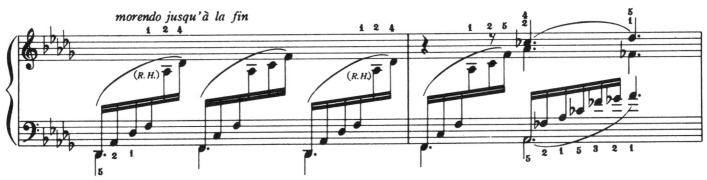

morendo jusqu'à la fin

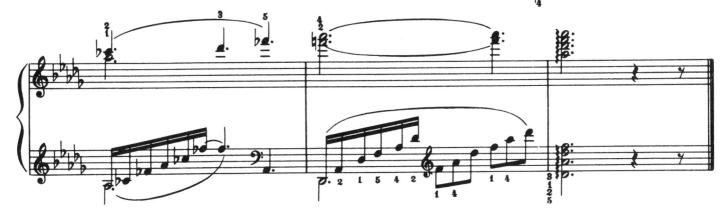

La Fille aux Cheveux de Lin

from Preludes Book 1

Claude Debussy
(1862–1918)

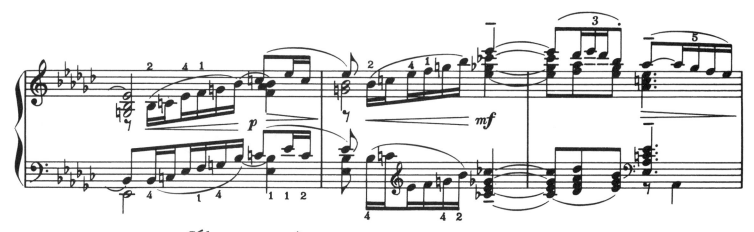

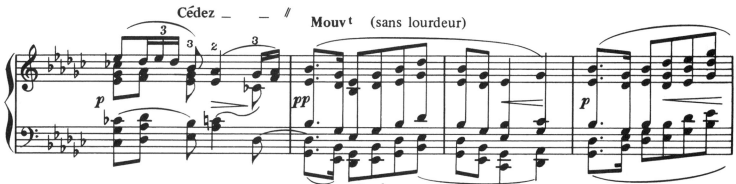

Cédez _ _ //   **Mouv**ᵗ (sans lourdeur)

très doux

Cédez _ // au **Mouv**ᵗ

Murmuré et en retenant peu à peu

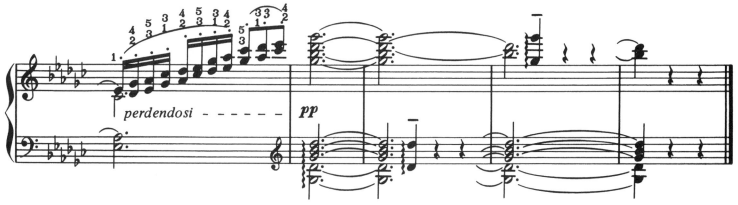

perdendosi - - - - - -   **pp**

Golliwog's Cake-walk

from Children's Corner

Claude Debussy
(1862–1918)

Un peu moins vite

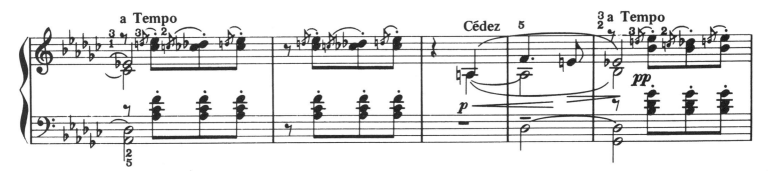

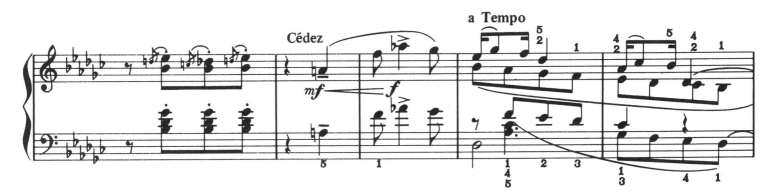

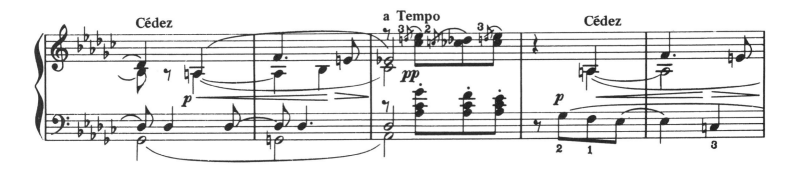

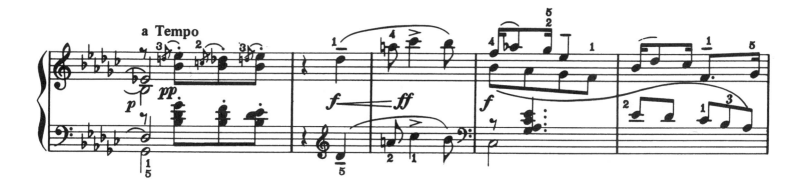

Deux Arabesques
1

Claude Debussy
(1862–1918)

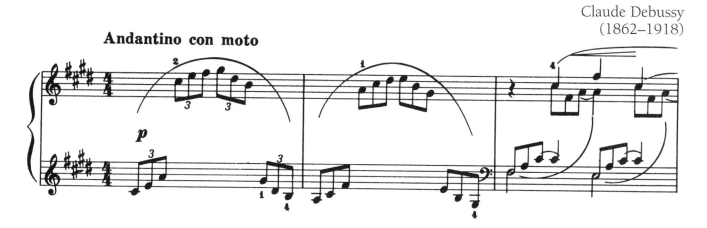

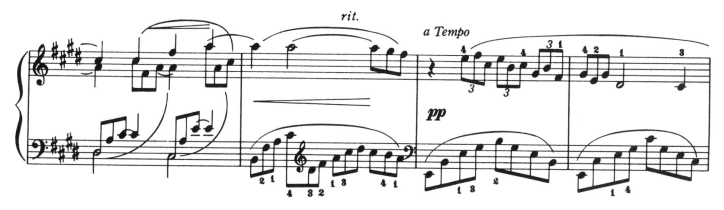

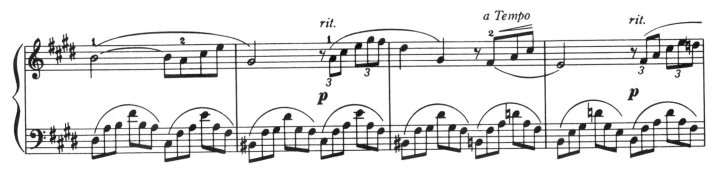

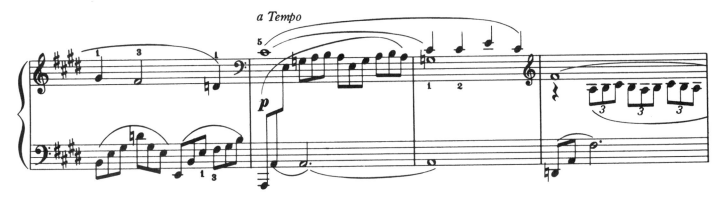

Tempo rubato (un peu moins vite)

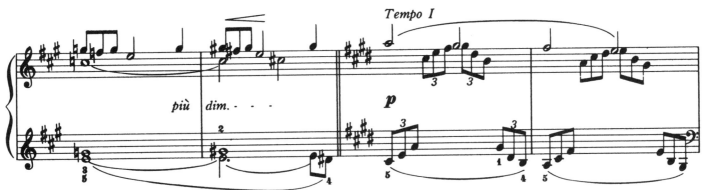

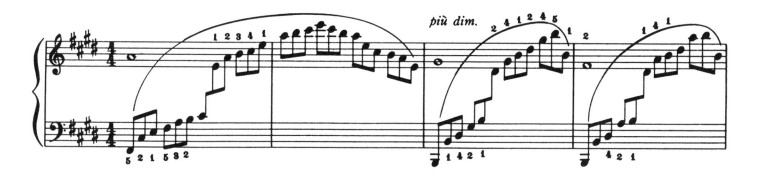

2

Allegretto scherzando

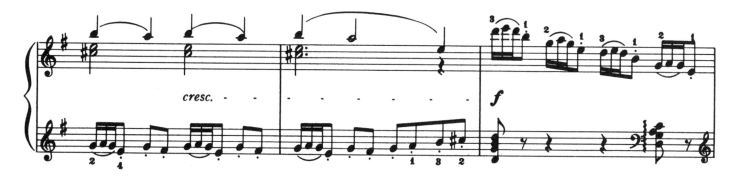

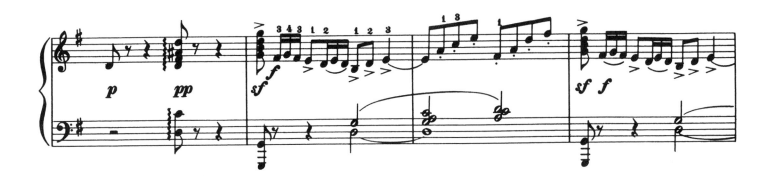

a Tempo

Humoresque

Op. 101, No. 7

Antonin Dvořák
(1841–1904)

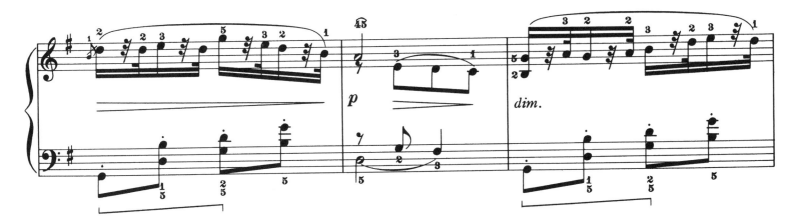

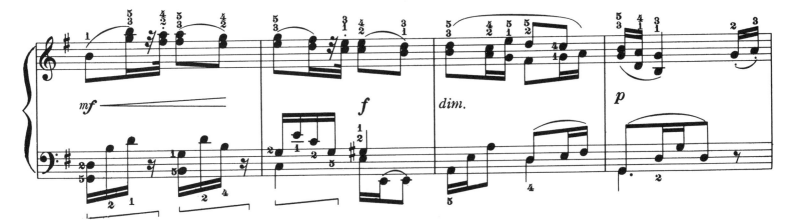

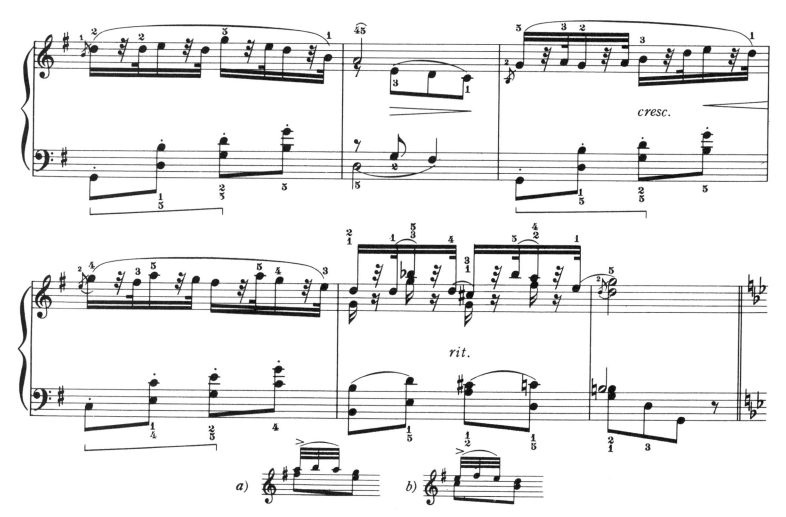

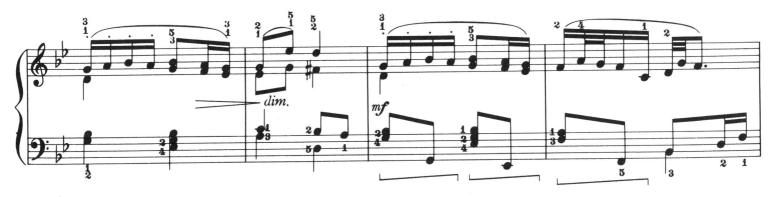

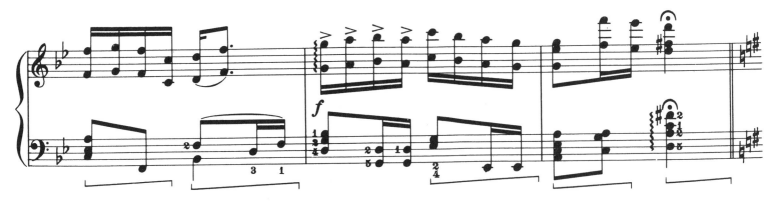

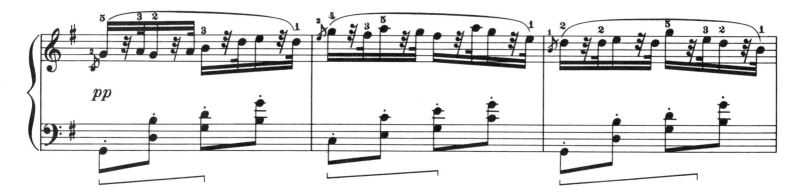

Nocturne

John Field
(1782–1837)

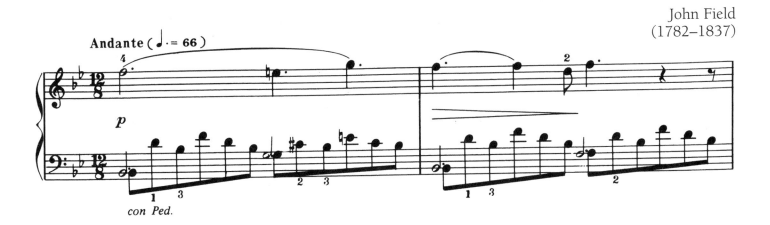

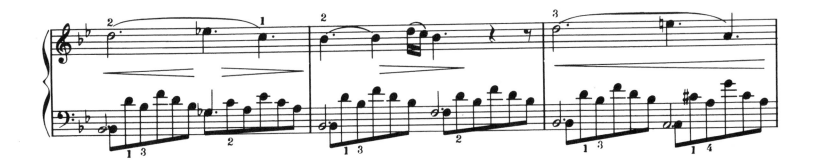

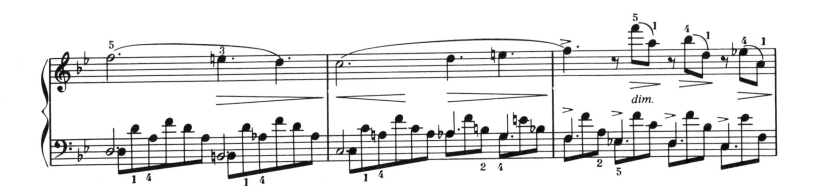

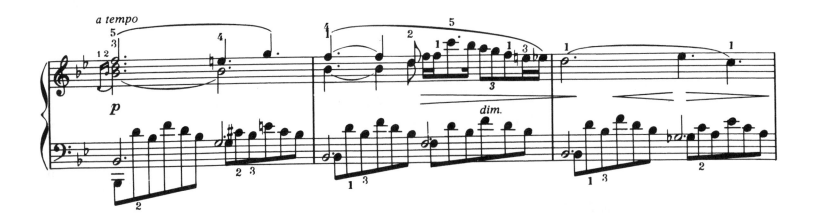

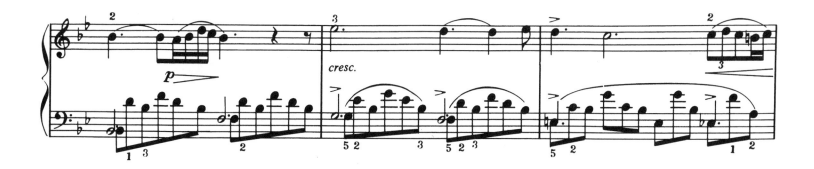

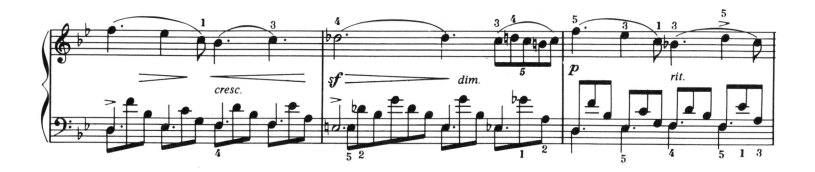

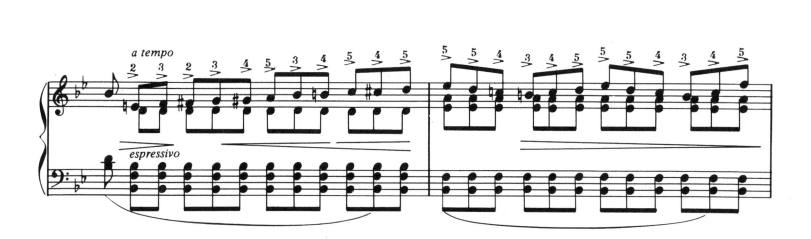

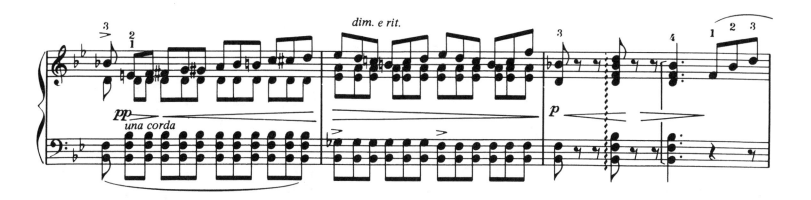

Tempo I°

mf espressivo   *pp*

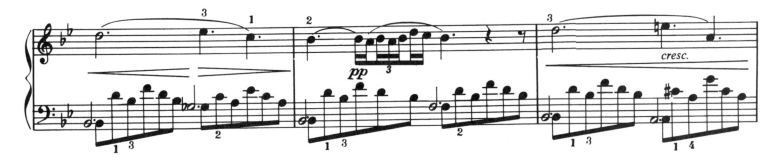

cresc.   *pp*

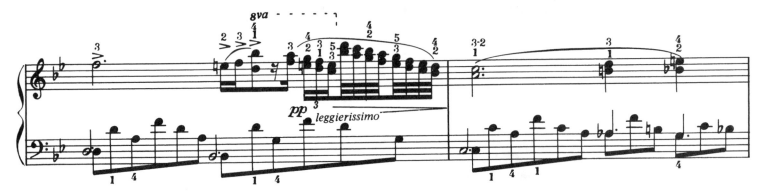

pp leggierissimo

cresc.   *sf*

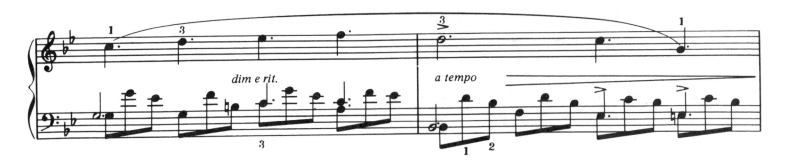

dim e rit.   *a tempo*

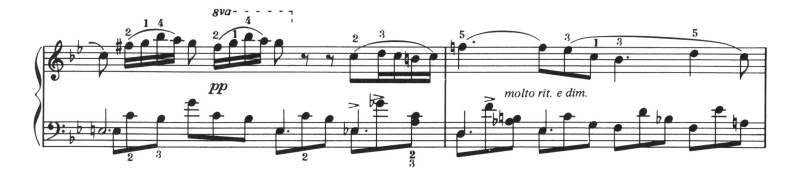

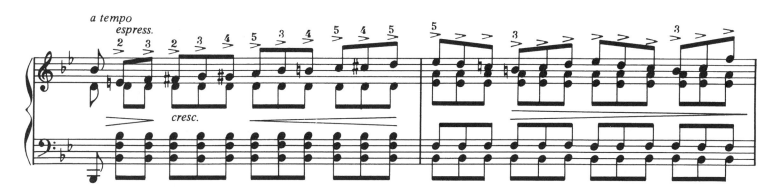

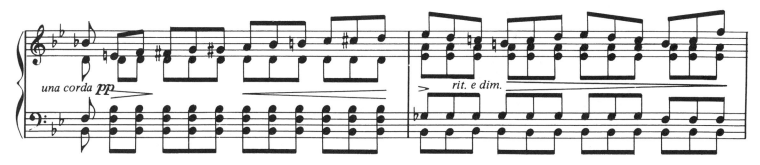

Anitra's Dance

from Peer Gynt

Edvard Grieg
(1843–1907)

Tempo di Mazurka. ♩ = 160.

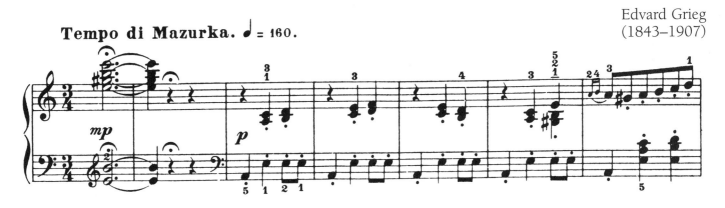

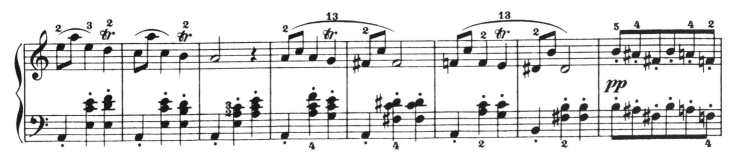

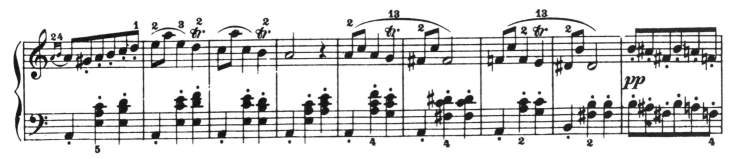

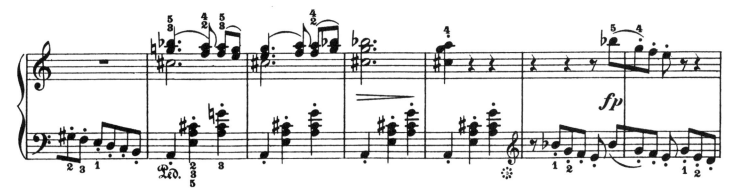

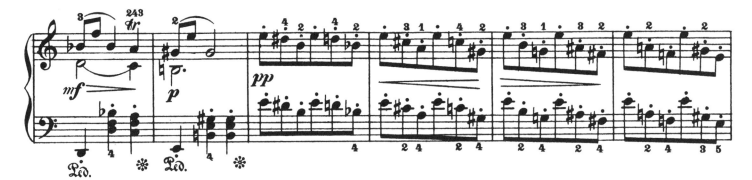

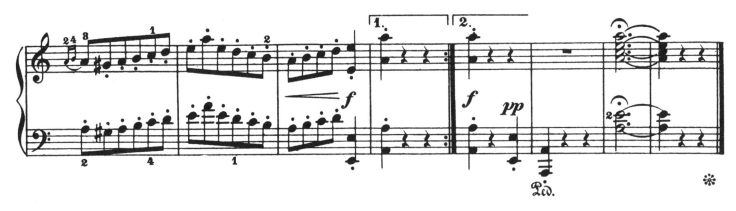

The Doll's Complaint

Le Plaintes d'une Poupée

César Franck
(1822–1890)

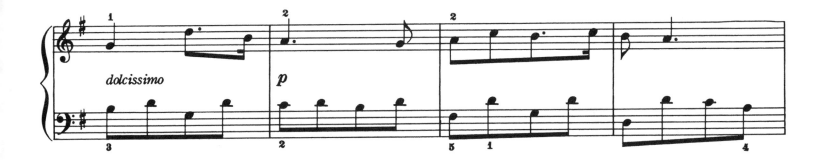

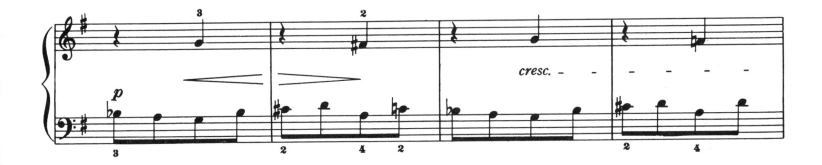

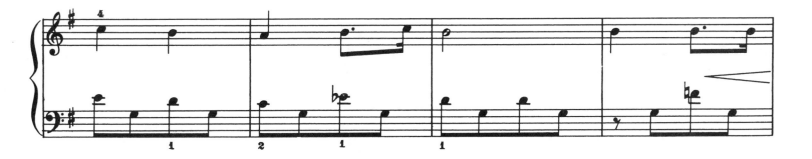

Gavotte in D

François Joseph Gossec
(1734–1829)

Poco allegro ma non troppo

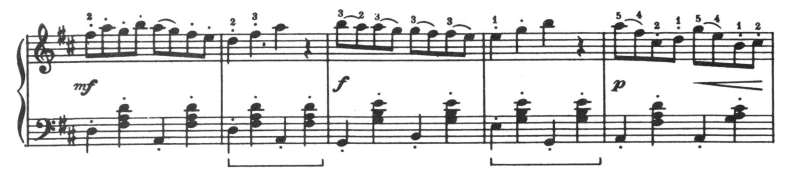

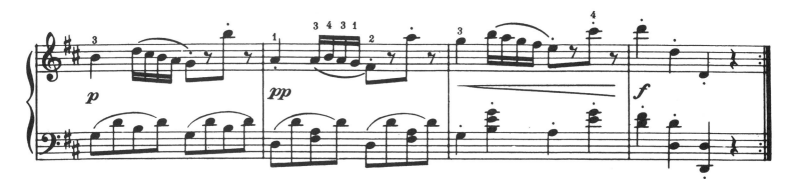

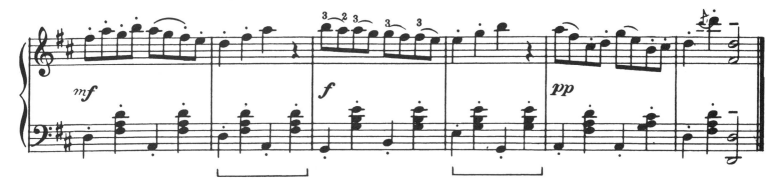

Air and Variations

The Harmonious Blacksmith from Suite No. 5

George Frideric Handel
(1685–1759)

Var. 2

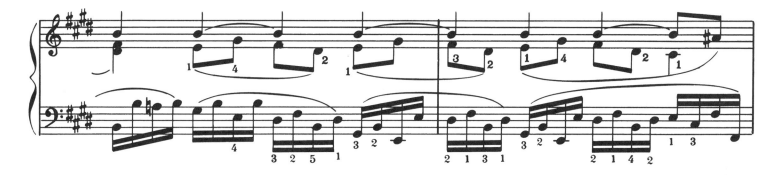

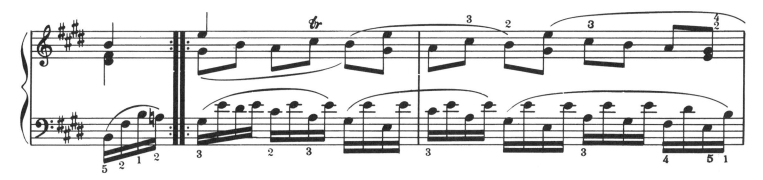

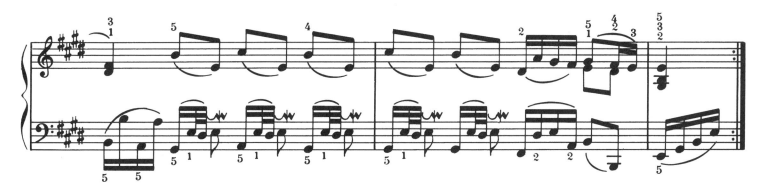

Var. 3

legato

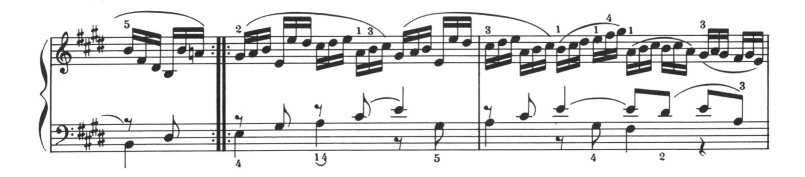

Var. 4

Var. 5

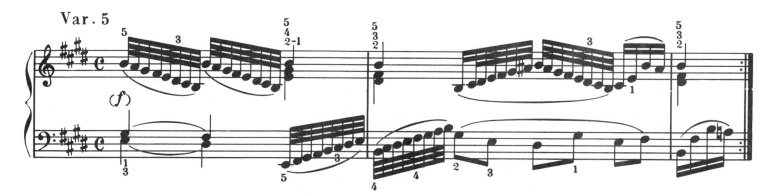

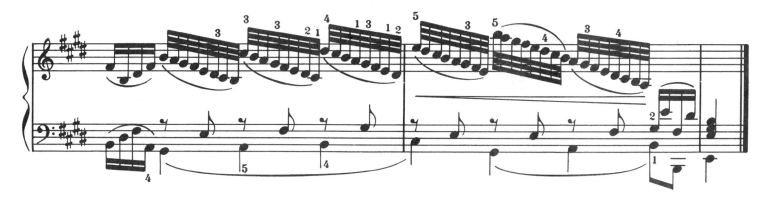

Largo

George Frideric Handel
(1685–1759)

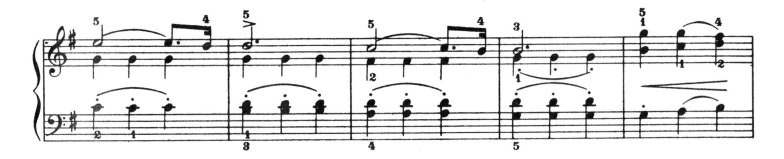

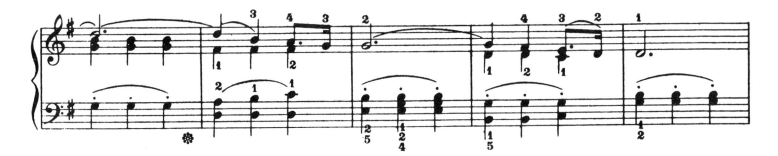

Humoresque

Edvard Grieg
(1843–1907)

Allegretto con grazia

Gypsy Rondo

Joseph Haydn
(1732–1809)

Minore I

Maggiore

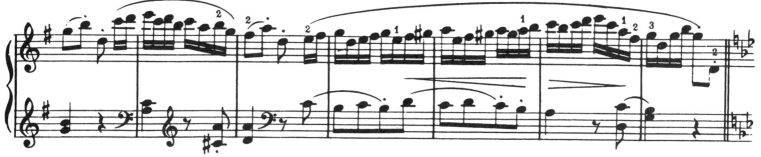

Minore II

Maggiore

The Cascades

A Rag

Scott Joplin
(1868–1917)

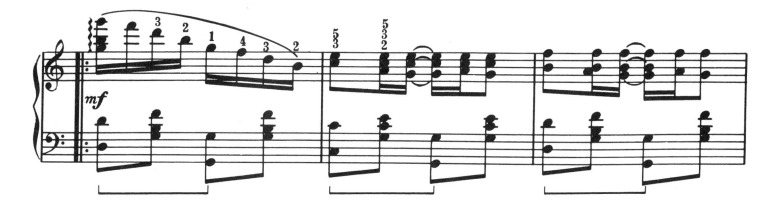

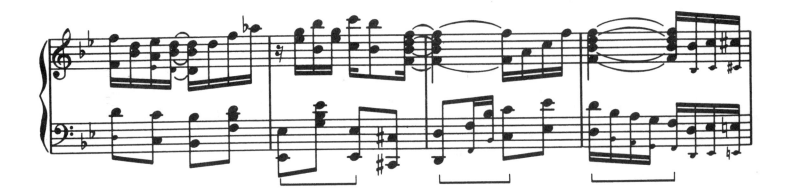

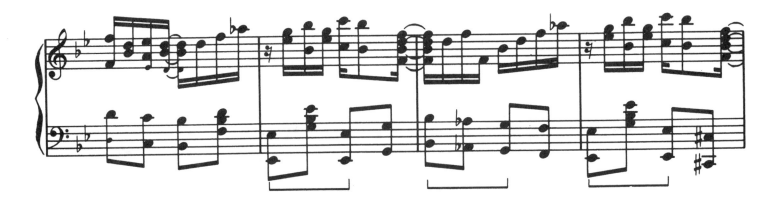

Having Fun

from Op. 27

Dmitri Kabalevsky
(1904–1987)

Vivace leggiero

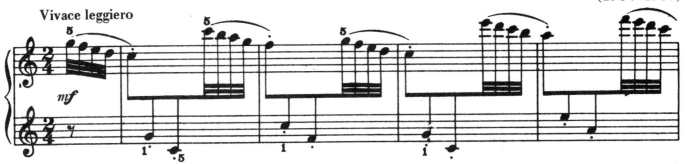

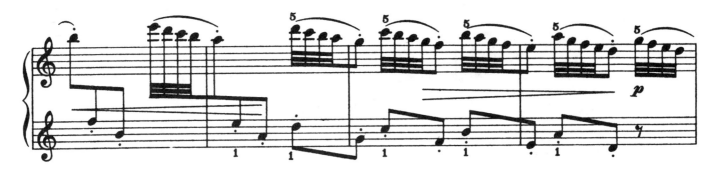

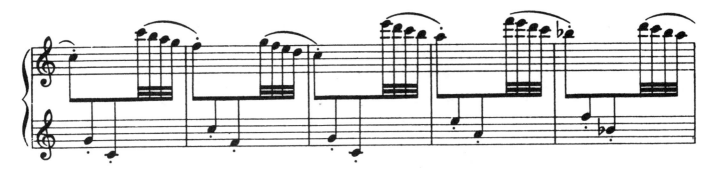

Saber Dance

from "Gayne Ballet"

Aram Khachaturian
(1903–1978)

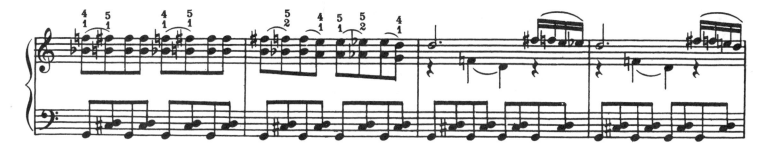

The Music Box

Op. 32

Anatol Liadov
(1855–1914)

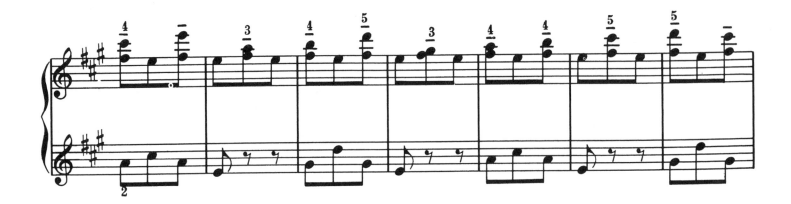

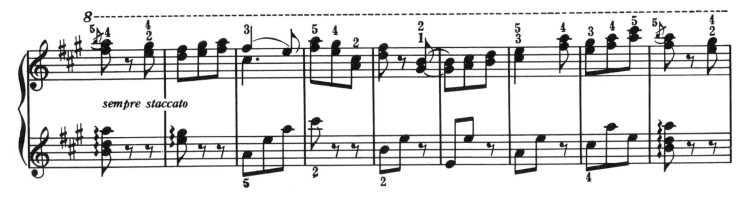

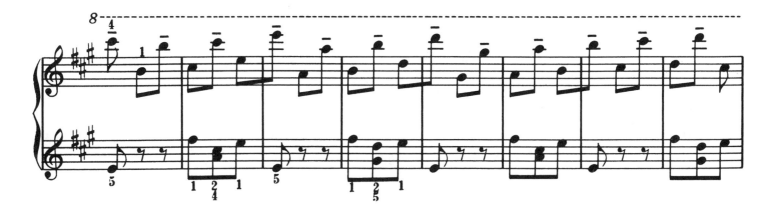

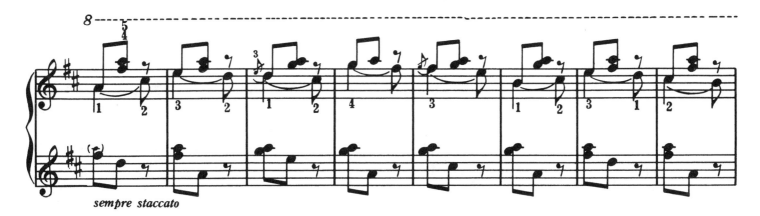

sempre staccato

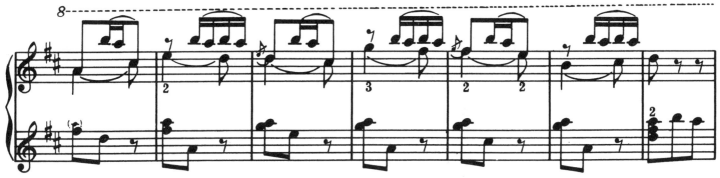

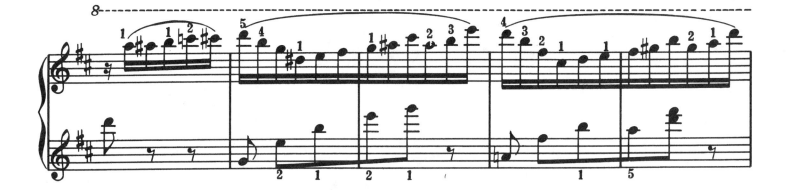

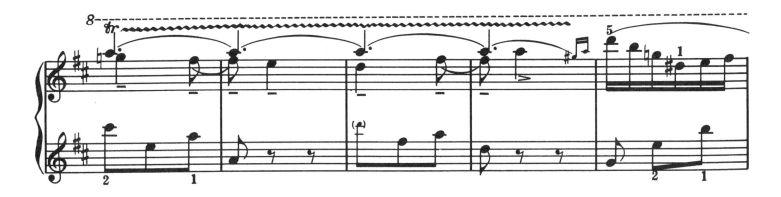

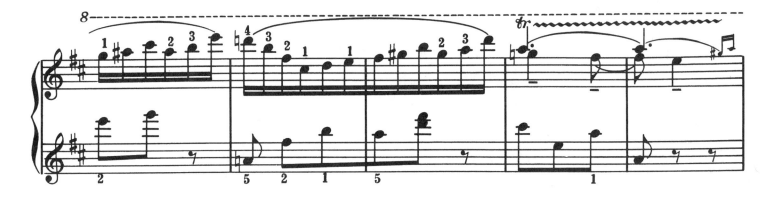

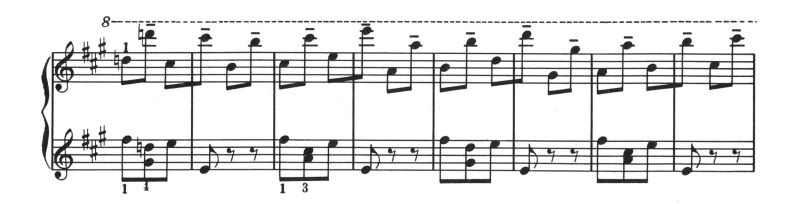

Liebestraum

Notturno No. 3

Franz Liszt
(1811–1886)

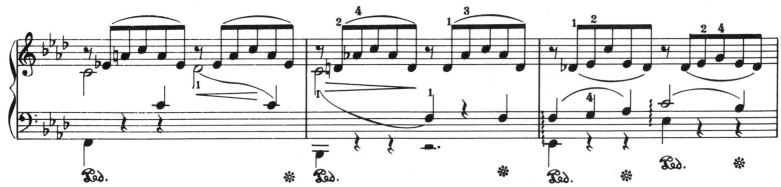

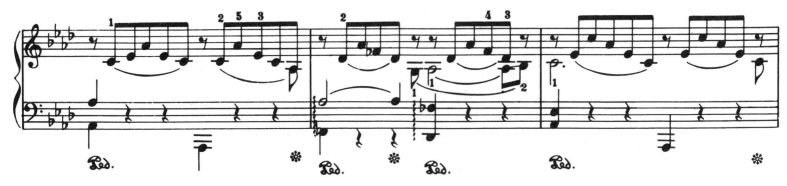

156

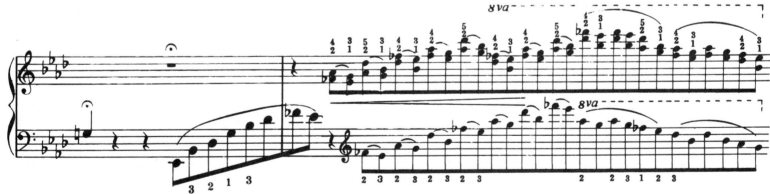

Più animato, con passione

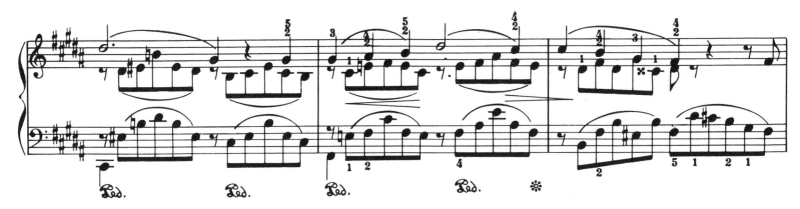

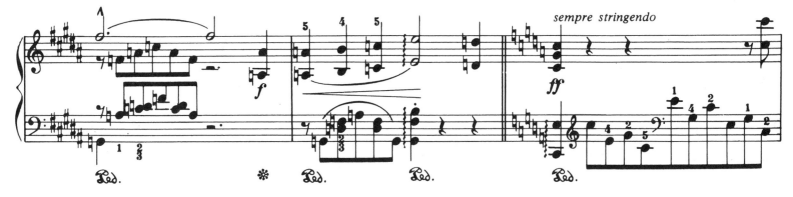

sempre stringendo

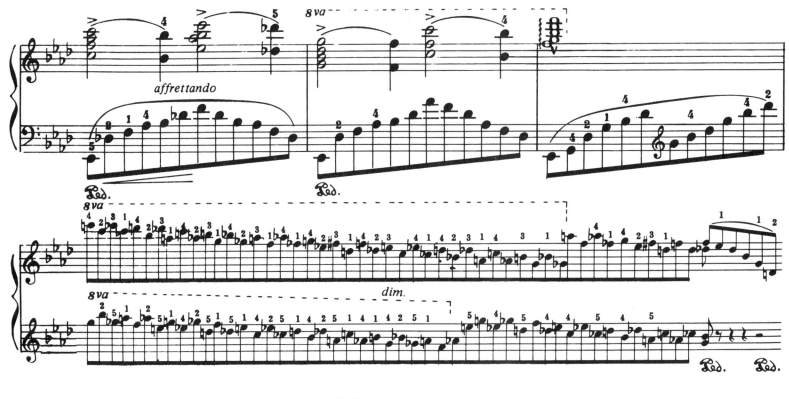

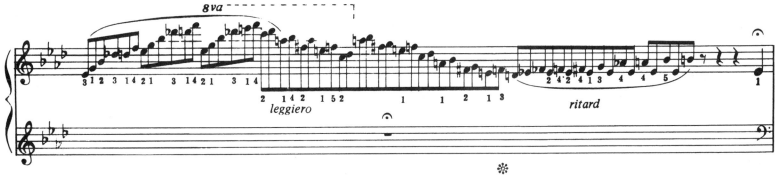

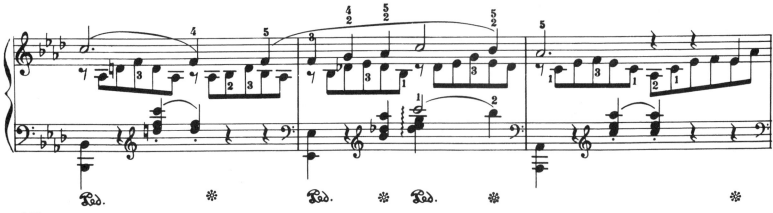

160

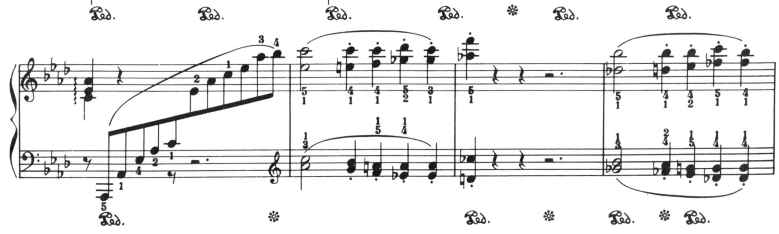

To a Wild Rose

Op. 51, No. 1

Edward MacDowell
(1860–1908)

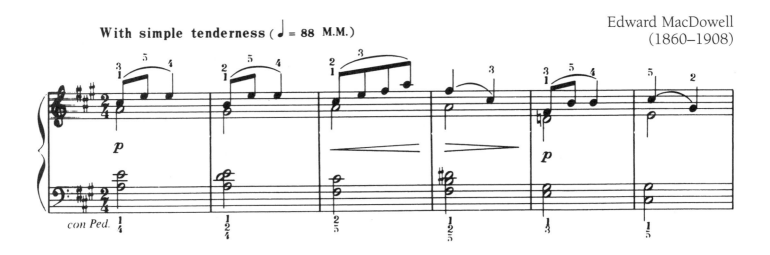

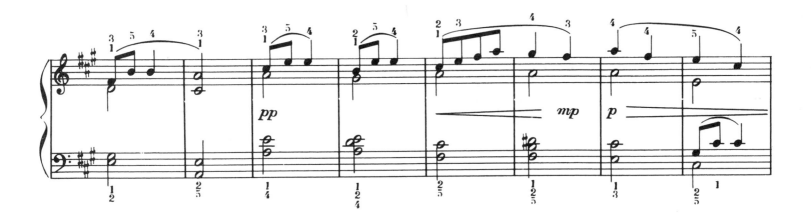

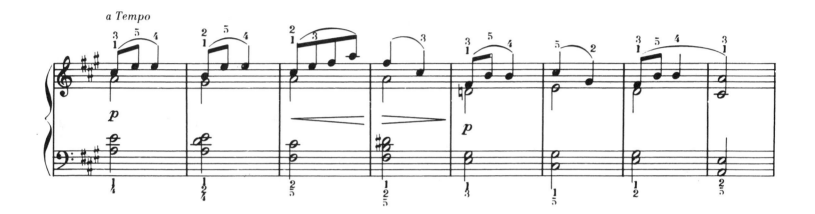

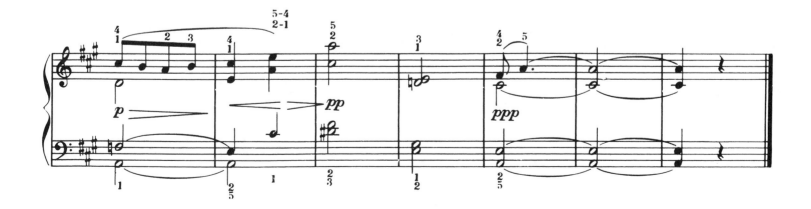

Elegie
Melodie Op. 10

Jules Massenet
(1842–1912)

Lento, ma non troppo

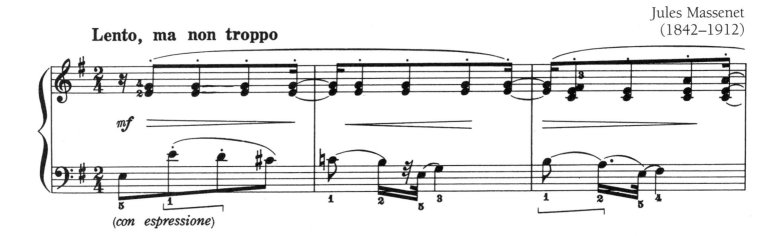

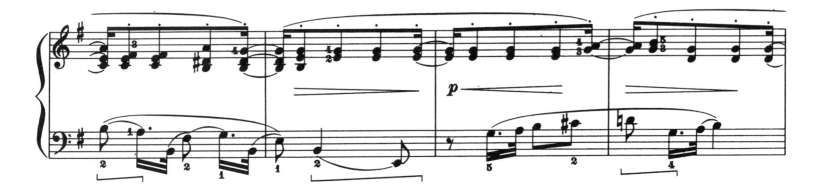

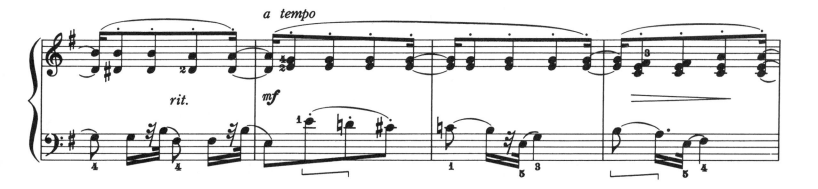

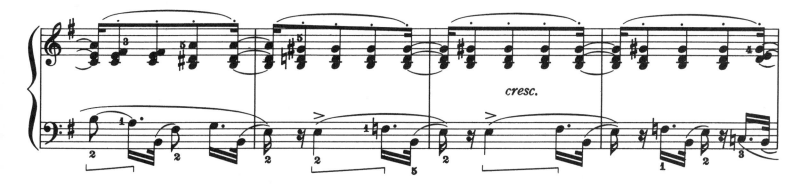

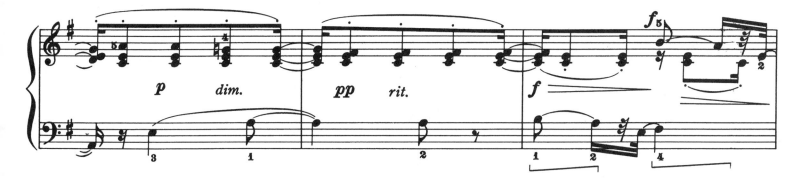

Venetian Boat Song

Op. 19, No.6

Felix Mendelssohn
(1809–1847)

Andante sostenuto

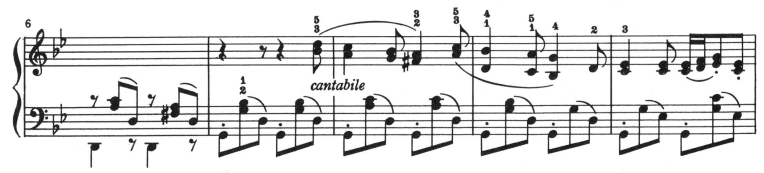

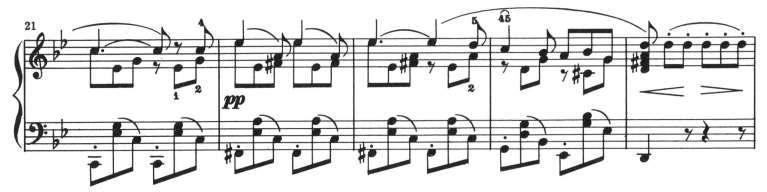

Alla Turca

from Sonata K. 331

Wolfgang Amadeus Mozart
(1756–1791)

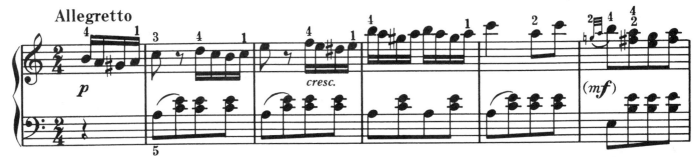

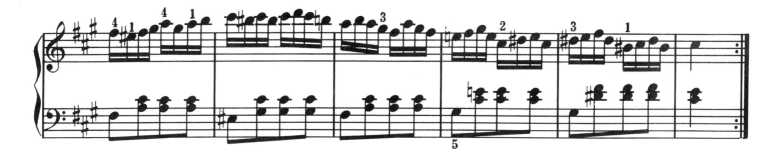

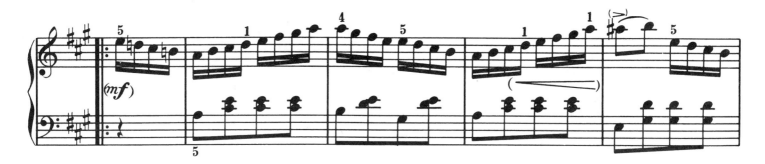

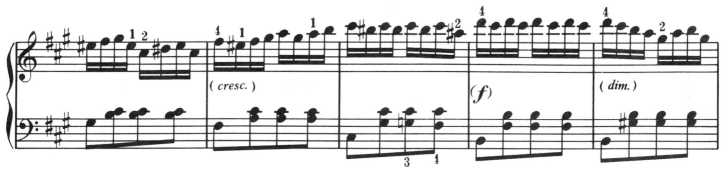

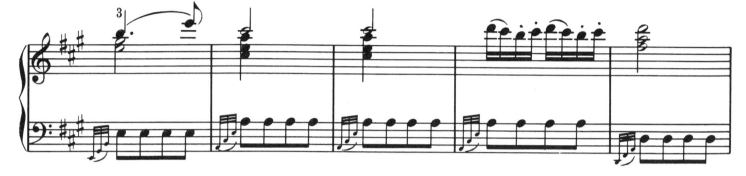

Sonata

K. 545

Wolfgang Amadeus Mozart
(1756–1791)

Andante

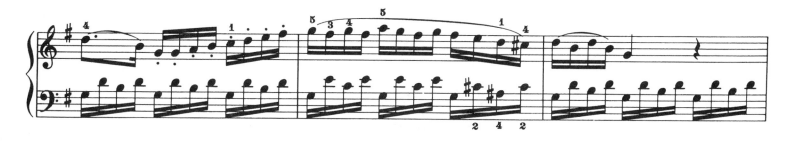

177

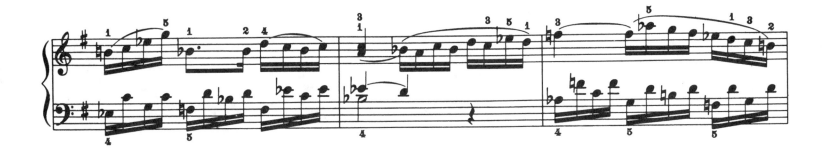

Rondo（Allegro）

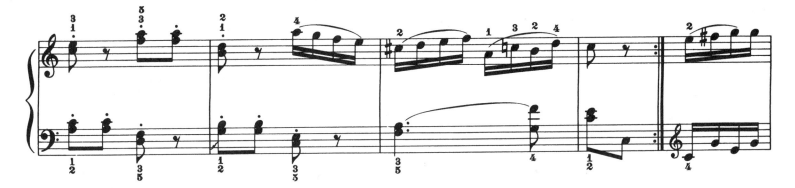

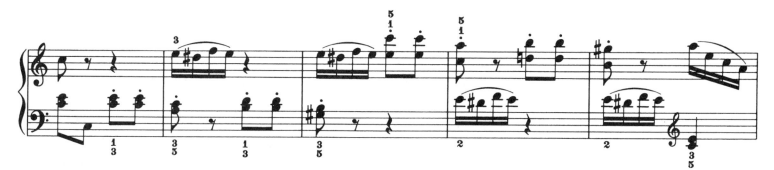

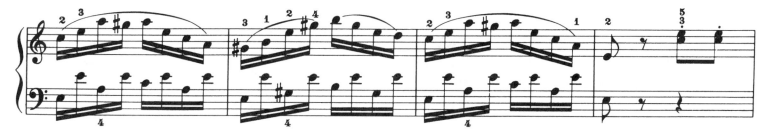

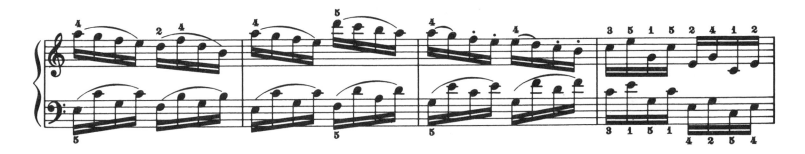

Fantasy in D Minor

K. 397

Wolfgang Amadeus Mozart
(1756–1791)

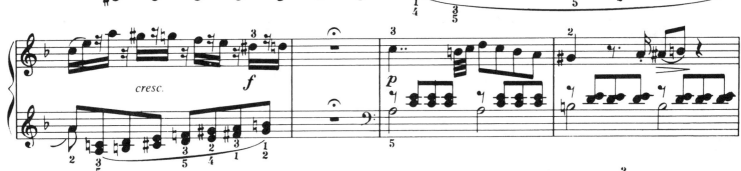

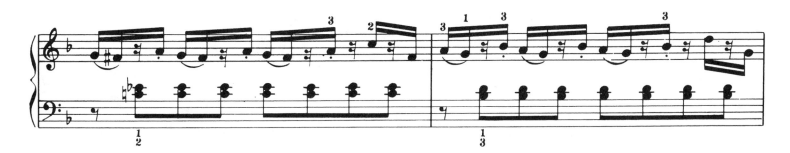

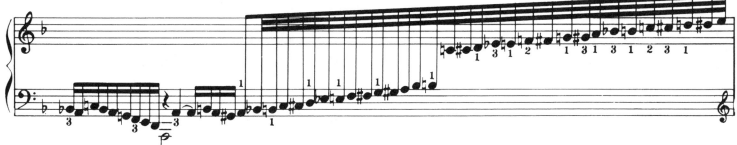

Allegretto

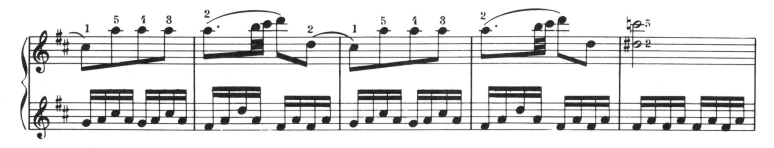

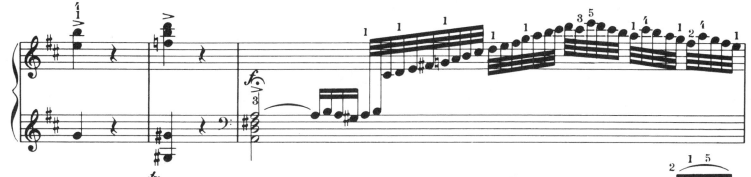

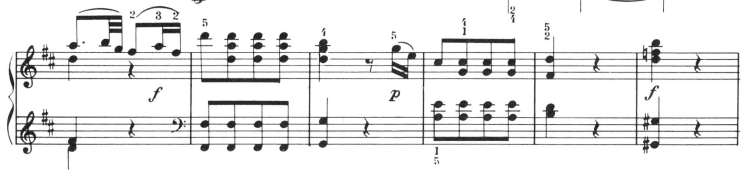

Rondo in D

K. 485

Wolfgang Amadeus Mozart
(1756–1791)

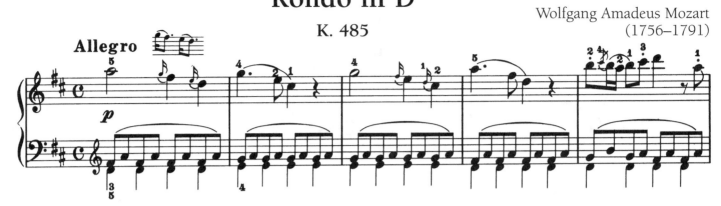

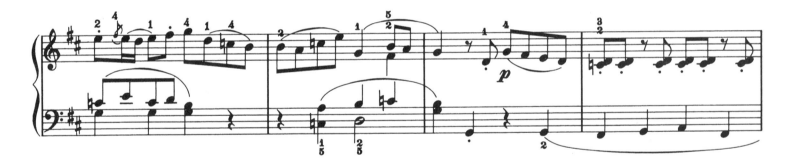

Barcarolle

from Tales of Hoffman

Jacques Offenbach
(1819–1880)

Peter and the Wolf

Sergei Prokofiev
(1891–1953)

Slow two beats

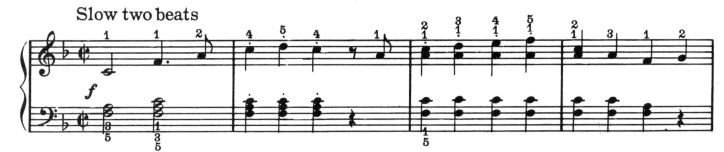

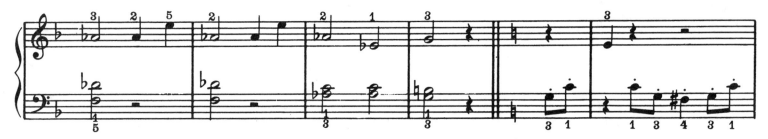

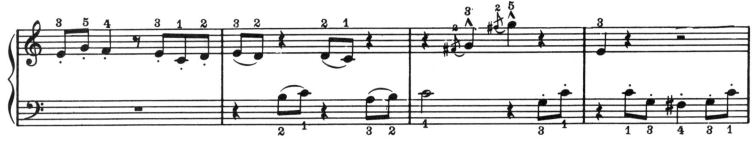

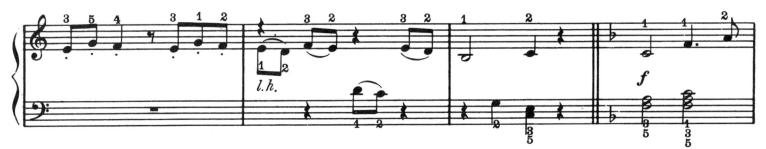

Prelude

Op. 32, No. 2

Sergei Rachmaninoff
(1873–1943)

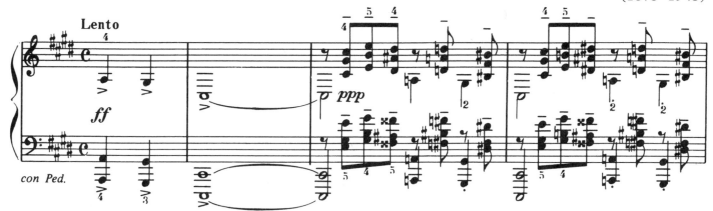

Agitato

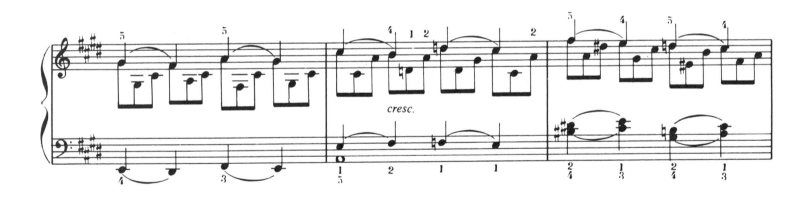

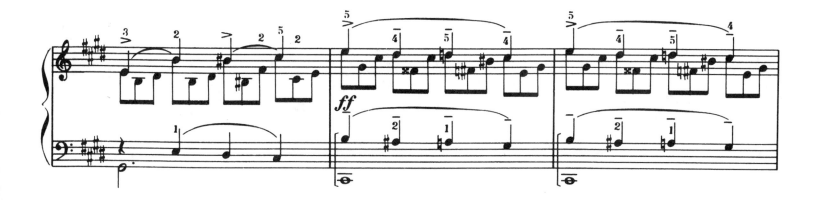

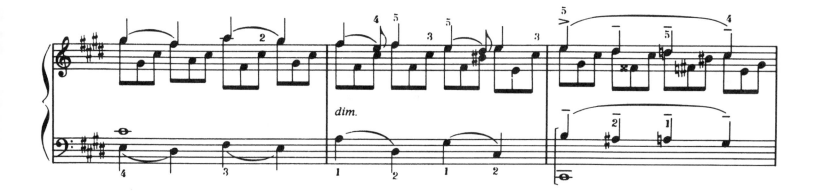

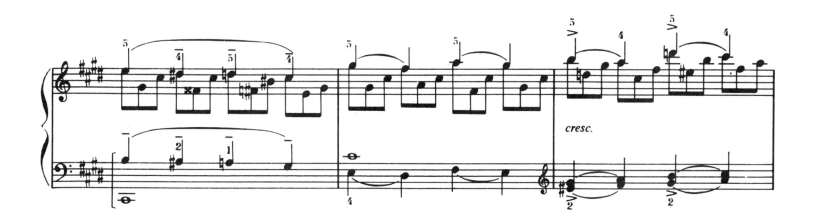

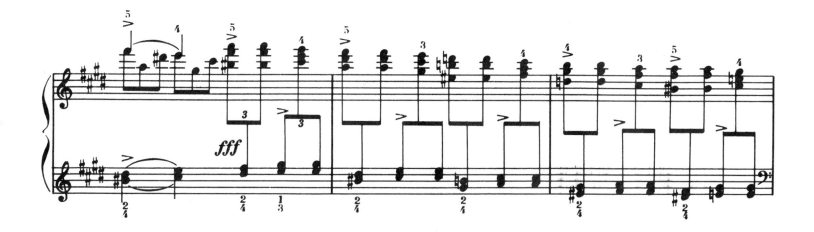

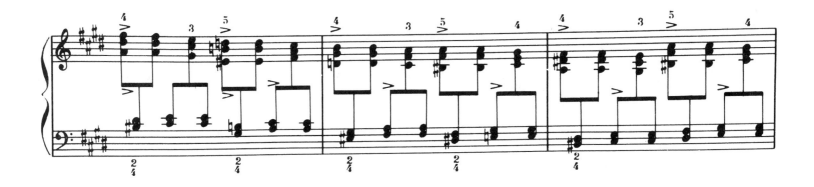

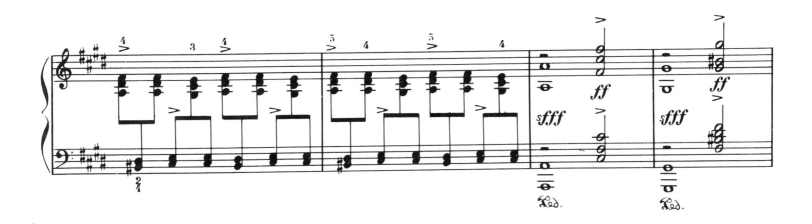

Tempo I°

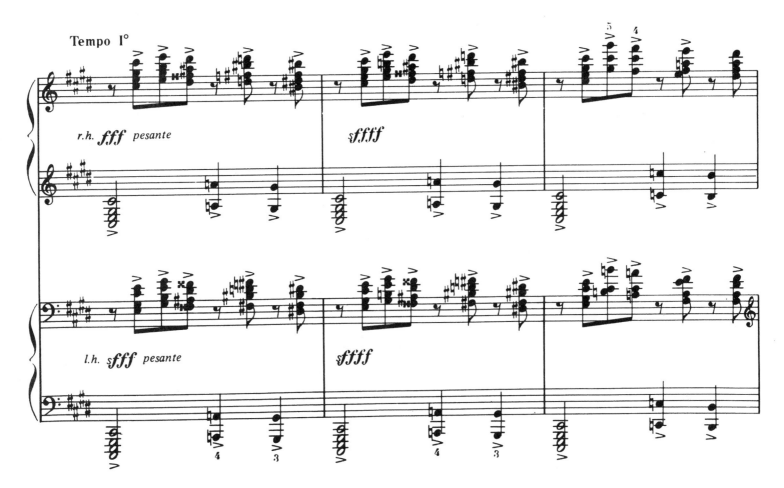

La Tambourin

Jean-Philippe Rameau
(1683–1764)

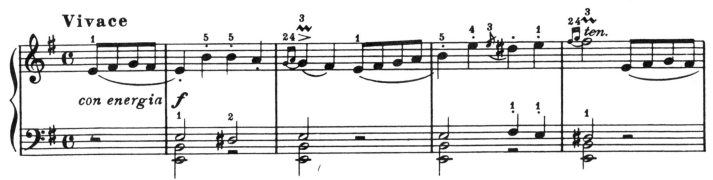

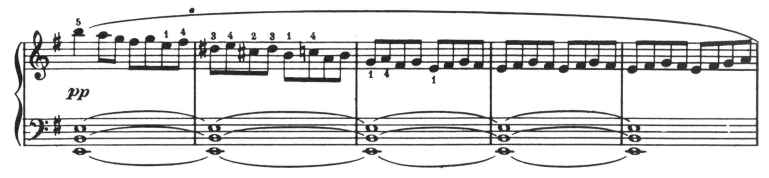

Song of India

Nikolay Rimsky-Korsakov
(1844–1908)

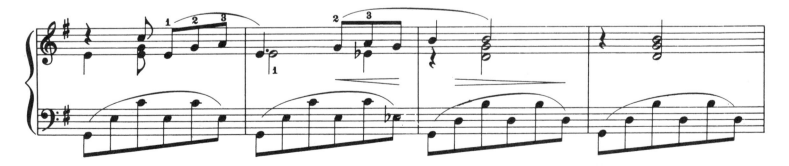

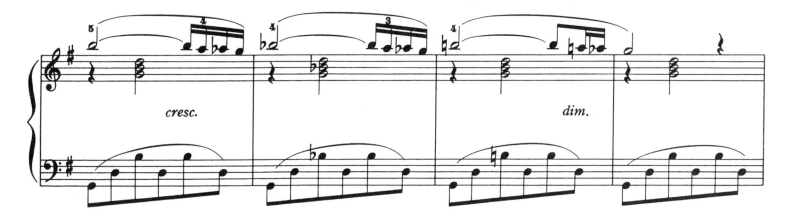

Trois Gnossiennes

Erik Satie
(1866–1925)

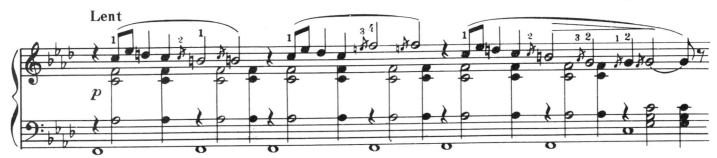

Du bout de la pensée

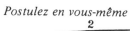

Postulez en vous-même

Pas à Pas

Sur la langue

2.

Avec étonnement

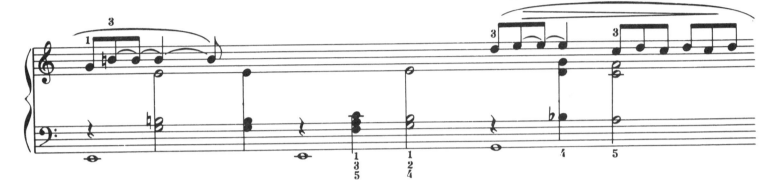

Ne sortez pas

Dans une grande bonté

Pius intimement

Avec une légère intimité

Sans orgueil

3.

Lent

Conseillez-vous soigneusement

Munissez-vous de clairvoyance

Seul, pendant un instant

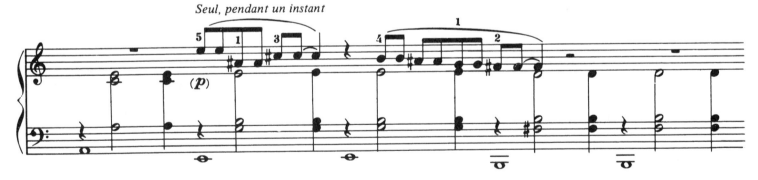

De manière à obtenir un creux

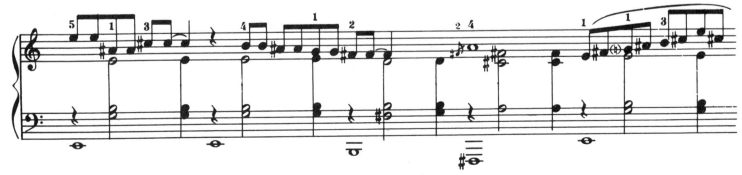

Très perdu

Portez cela plus loin

Ouvrez la tete

Enfouissez le son

Sonata

L. 375

Domenico Scarlatti
(1685–1757)

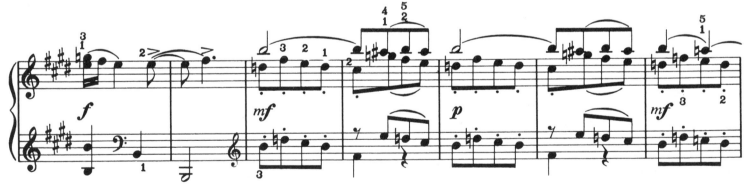

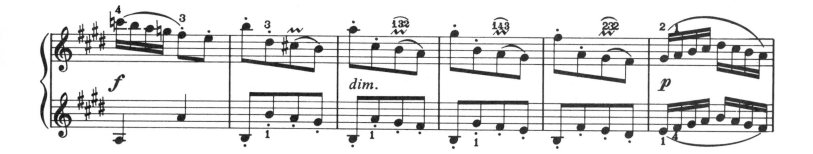

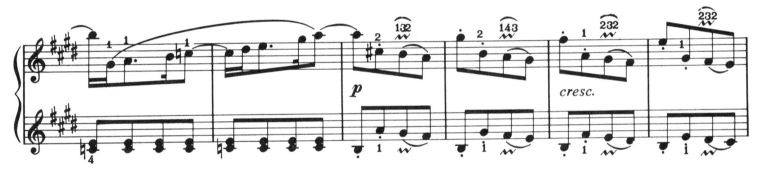

Italian Song

Op. 39, No. 15

Peter I. Tchaikovsky
(1840–1893)

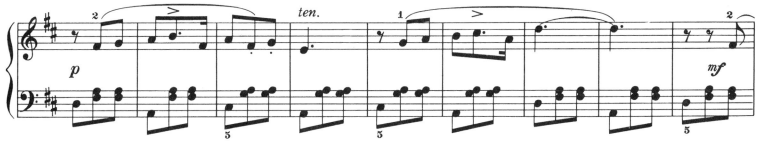

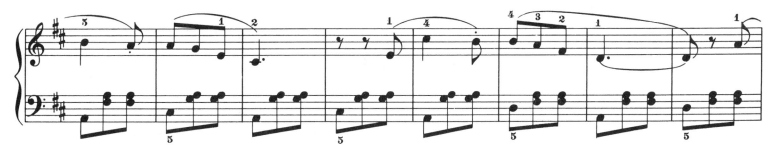

Album Leaf

Op. 45, No. 1

Alexander Scriabin
(1872–1915)

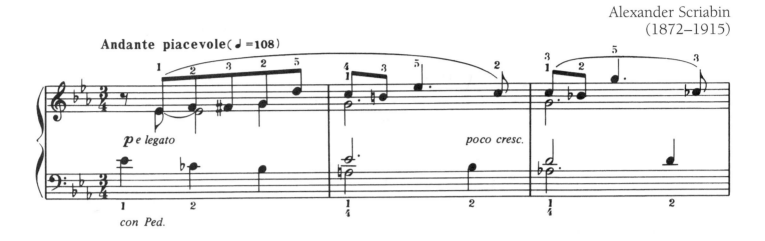

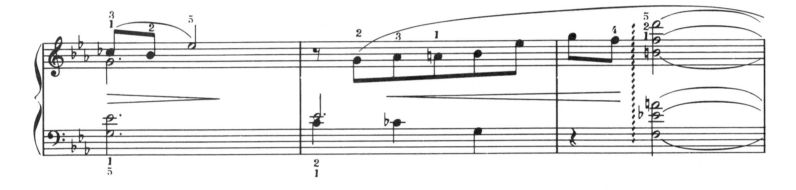

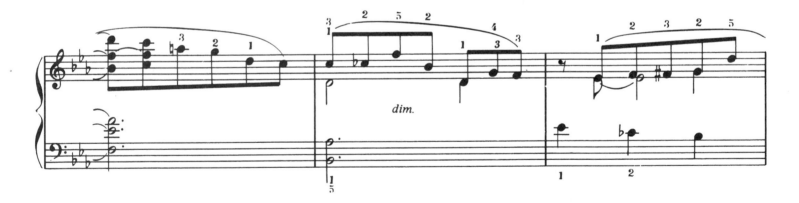

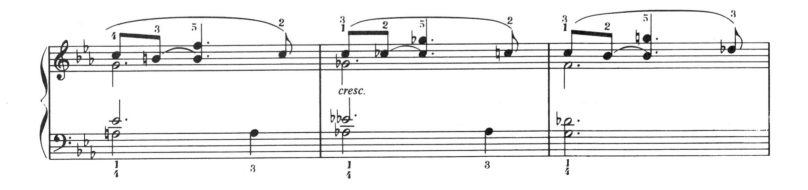

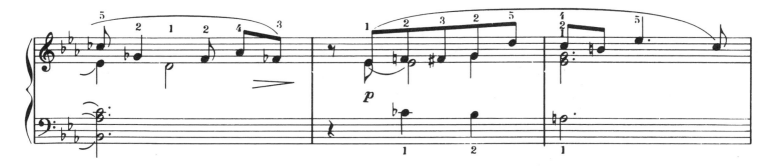

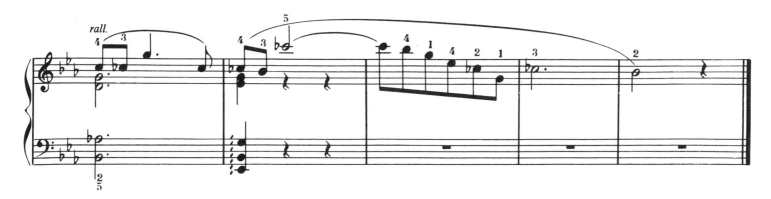

Polka

from The Golden Age Ballet

Dmitri Shostakovitch
(1906–1975)

Allegretto

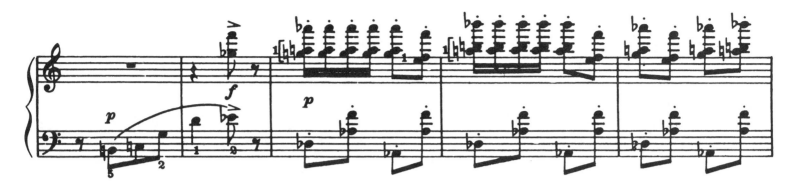

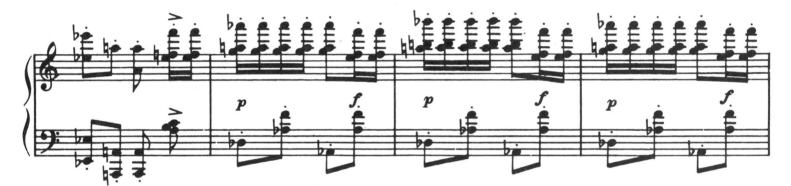

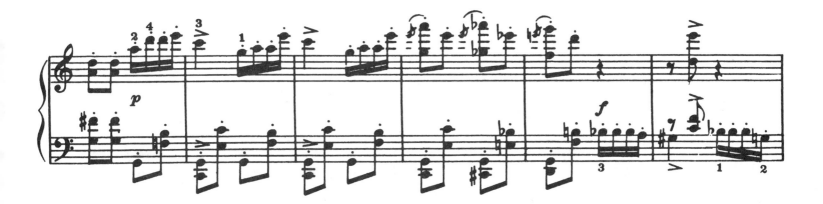

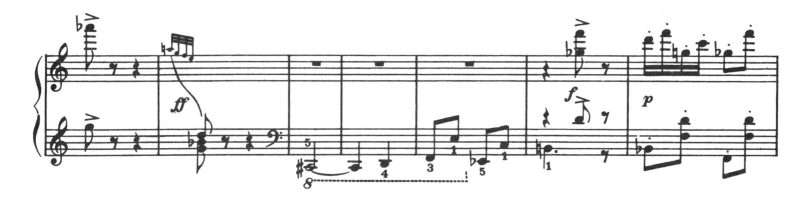

Serenade

Franz Schubert
(1797–1828)

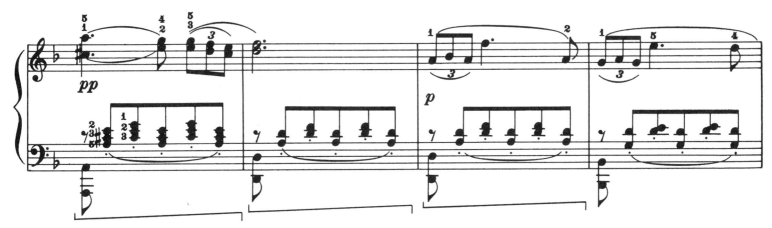

Ped. simile
a tempo

Moment Musical

Op. 94, No. 3

Franz Schubert
(1797–1828)

Allegro moderato

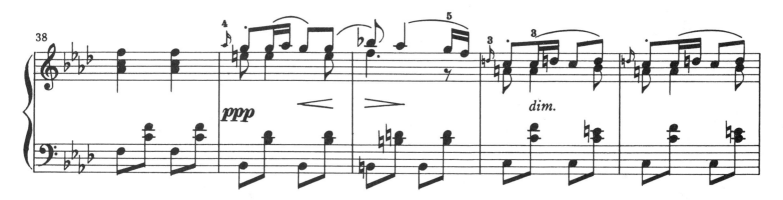

Marche Militaire

Op. 51, No. 1

Franz Schubert
(1797–1828)

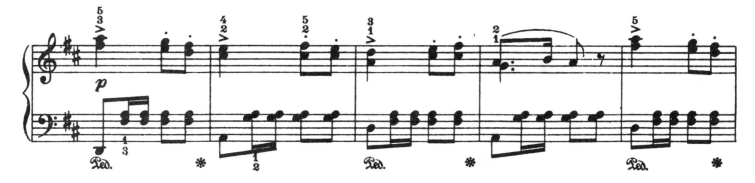

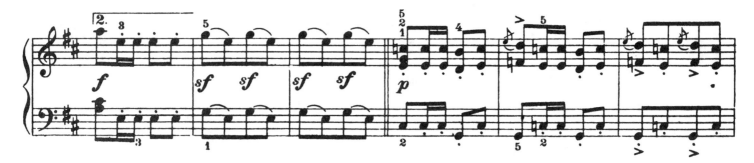

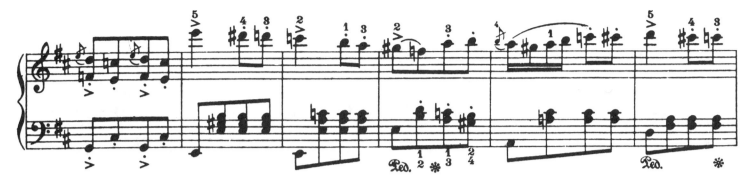

Trio

Marcia D.C. al Fine

Soldiers' March

from Album for the Young

Robert Schumann
(1810–1856)

Munter und straff (*gay but strict*)

The Beautiful Blue Danube

Tempo di Valse

Johann Strauss II
(1825–1899)

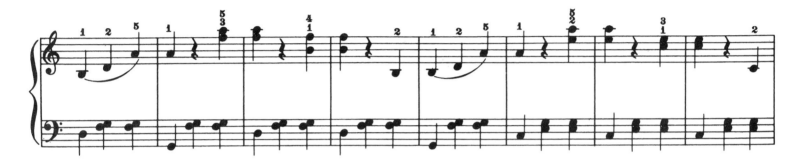

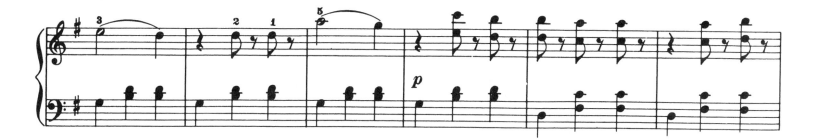

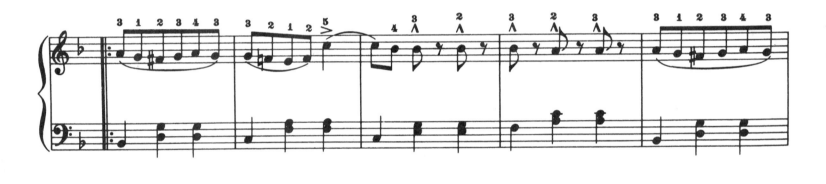

236

Coda

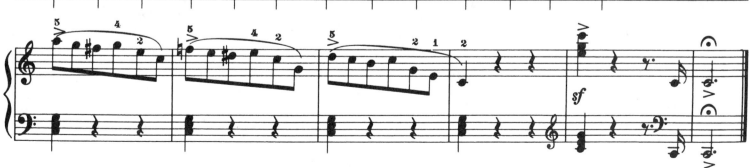

Waltz

Carl Maria von Weber
(1786–1826)

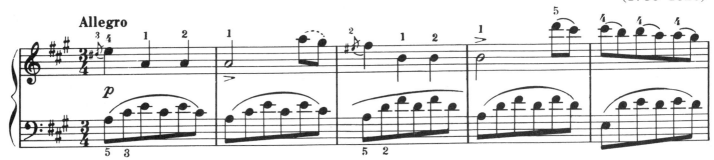

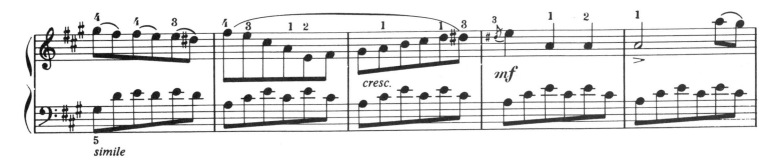

Träumerei

Robert Schumann
(1810–1856)

Moderato (♩=100)